D1495519

Desirée Mays

Opera Unveiled

2005

♪

ART FORMS INC.
Santa Fe · Salt Lake City

Cover design and layout by Pieter Hull
Rear cover photograph by Carolyn Wright

First edition

ISBN 0-9707822-4-1

To order copies of *Opera Unveiled 1999 - 2005*
please send a check for $15 (postage included) to:
Art Forms, Inc., 31 Valencia Loop
Santa Fe, New Mexico 87508
Fax: (505) 466 1908
Email: dmmays@gmail.com

Contents

Cover: "*Arlecchino*" circa 1700
artist unknown

Turandot

Giacomo Puccini

Turandot is an enigmatic fairytale with mythic overtones whose spell has endured over the centuries. The composer of the opera *Turandot*, Giacomo Puccini, struggled to give birth to his final creation, struggled with its composition, and struggled mightily with its ending. But he was ultimately defeated by what he hoped would be the crowning achievement of his career, and had to leave the opera where he had finished all his earlier operas – with the death of the suffering heroine, for Puccini's struggle with the icy Princess ended with his own death. His pages of unfinished notes and sketches for the opera's closing love duet and finale were left to be completed by another composer.

Having premiered *Il Trittico*, his trilogy of one-act operas, in January 1919, Giacomo Puccini searched for a source for his next opera. He told his librettists, Renato Simoni and Giuseppe Adami, that he wanted to "strike out on new paths with a fantastic, fairytale subject that was both human and moving." Adami, a noted playwright, had written the libretti for Puccini's *La Rondine* and *Il Tabarro*; Simoni, a dramatist and editor for a time of Milan's leading evening paper, *Il Corriere della Sera*, had just written an account of his travels in Asia and was a Gozzi scholar. Over lunch one summer's day in Milan in 1920, the three men settled on the tale of Turandot.

Count Gozzi's *Turandotte* (1762) is a tragicomedy based on the ancient Persian legend of a cruel Chinese princess who was transformed when she found true love – a classic tale of love and hate that immediately appealed to Puccini. In his play, Gozzi embodied the virtues of courage, loyalty, strength in suffering, and self-sacrifice in the characters of the Unknown Prince and his father, Timur, exiled king of the Tartars. Gozzi also injected incongruous comic elements into his play by featuring fantastic characters from the world of the commedia dell'arte. In Puccini's opera, these stock comic characters, known in Italy as the Venetian Masks, evolved into the three Ministers, Ping, Pang, and Pong. Puccini had doubts about including them at first, but then told his librettists they were to be "philosophers and clowns, throwing in a comic remark here and there, but they must never demand too much attention." In fact, Puccini's Masks became major players in *Turandot*: grotesque, sinister characters of black humor who only occasionally show human traits of compassion and regret, in a nostalgia for home and their collective longing for a peaceful China. Puccini transformed Gozzi's fantastic little tale on many levels: in a grand heroic style with Turandot and the Unknown Prince; in a lyric and sentimental style expressed by the slave girl Liù, a character of Puccini's invention; in the comic-grotesque style of the Masks; and in the cruelty of the bloodthirsty crowd.

While composing *Turandot*, Puccini pestered his librettists, requiring endless revisions and often not waiting for them to respond before composing to words of his own. Despite such impatience, progress was slow and difficult. He instructed Simoni and Adami to "heighten the passion of Turandot, who has been buried for so long in the ashes of her great pride." The composer was plagued by self-doubt. He wrote to Adami, "Shall I be able to do my part? I am very much afraid. I am an old, abject, unhappy, discouraged man. What am I to do? I don't know." But later, he wrote, "*Turandot* is groaning and travailing, but pregnant with music." He composed Act I between spring and fall of 1922, completed Act II a little over a year later, and by March 1924, Act III had been composed up to the death of Liù. By September, the entire opera had been composed and orchestrated – all but the final duet between Calaf and Turandot and the Finale, neither of which Puccini lived to complete.

Turandot was a departure from Puccini's former works both in content and musical approach. He researched and wove a number of authentic Chinese melodies into the score, and included percussion instruments such as the triangle, glockenspiel, celesta, xylophone, and Chinese gongs in new orchestral combinations. For much of the score he used the five-note pentatonic scale to create an atmosphere of dissonance, but frequently reverted to soaring, whole-scale Italian melodies. The influences of Debussy, Massenet, Richard Strauss, and Stravinsky can all be found in this final work; *Turandot* is, by far, Puccini's most musically advanced opera.

Puccini transports us to an exotic place, to ancient China, a world in which Turandot appears out of the mists of time, beautiful, cold, unattainable, lethal. To brave and eligible princes of the ancient world, Turandot represented an irresistible challenge: she would marry the prince who could answer three riddles, but any suitor who failed to solve the riddles would be put to death.

The opera begins in the palace of the Emperor Altoum, in the Imperial City of Peking. The last rays of the setting sun bleakly illuminate the stage, which is typically divided among three levels. The highest, suggesting heaven itself, is the domain of the Emperor. The middle region is the level of Turandot, the courtiers, the three ministers Ping, Pang, and Pong, and the eight sages, who keep the scrolls that contain the answers to Turandot's riddles. On the lowest level are the people, the voice of China, which suffers cruelly under Turandot's decree – the country is uneasy and blood is the order of the day. The mood is dark, threatening, and somber.

There is no overture, no preparation for or warning of what is to come – Puccini thrusts us into ancient China with four unsettling, declamatory chords. The people are already assembling to hear the pronouncement of the Mandarin, who explains that Turandot the Chaste will be the bride of the man of royal blood who can answer three riddles; if he fails, he will die. The music supporting this pronouncement is bitonal, punctuated by Chinese gong and xylophone. The crowd seethes, restless, vengeful, intoxicated, eager for the next execution. They call for the executioner, Pu-Tin-Pao, for the Prince of Persia is to die at the rising of the moon. On poles along the walls of the palace can be seen the impaled heads of former princes, unsuccessful suitors from many lands.

The mood of barbaric cruelty is interrupted when, in the midst of the crowd, an old man stumbles and falls. His companion, Liù, a mere girl, tries to lift him. When she asks for help, a young man goes to the fallen man's side, and instantly the two recognize one another – the old man is Timur, the exiled king of Tartary, and the younger is his son, Calaf, the Unknown Prince. Both men fear for their lives, yet are overjoyed to be reunited. The oblivious crowd swarms around them, calling for the death of the Prince of Persia as the executioner sharpens his great sword.

"Liù, who are you?" asks the Unknown Prince. "I am nothing; a slave, my lord," she replies. When Calaf asks her why she endures such anguish, she says, "I endure it because one day, in the palace, you smiled at me." This simple statement reveals the extraordinary devotion and fortitude that motivates Liù, a young woman, to accompany her king, an old man, on a hopeless journey of exile. "There is no refuge for us," Calaf tells his father.

The mood of the crowd reaches fever pitch. In a frenzy, they sing repeatedly that "The riddles are three, death is one." They direct their impatience at the moon: "Why does the moon delay? Show yourself! Rise! O bloodless one, pale lover of the dead." We are reminded of the opening measures of Strauss's *Salome*: "See the moon's pale disk, it has such a strange look, like a woman rising from the grave."

The chill whiteness of the rising moon fills the stage as the guards appear, leading the bareheaded Prince of Persia, a handsome young man who walks as if in a dream. Behind him looms the gigantic executioner, his gleaming sword on his shoulder. When the crowd sees the condemned Prince, they quickly change their cries to pleas for Turandot's pity. Witnessing this scene, the Unknown Prince leads the cry: "Cruel one, let me curse you!"

As if summoned by his cry, Turandot appears high above – a vision moonlit, beautiful, majestic, all-powerful – to a glorious theme based on "Moo-lee-wah," a traditional Chinese melody. The crowd falls to its knees; the Unknown Prince is transfixed by Turandot's beauty. "O divine beauty, O wonder," he cries out. Surrounded by her women, the silent princess does not sing, but raises her hand and makes an imperious gesture of death. The executioner nods, the procession moves slowly offstage, and Turandot disappears. The ecstatic Calaf stands speechless with wonder. Timur and Liù beg him to leave this dangerous place, but he sees only Turandot and is determined to stay. He moves toward the great gong to announce his intention but is held back by the sudden appearance of three strange characters.

Ping, Pang, and Pong, ministers of the court, insist that Calaf leave. "Madman, this is the gate to the great butcher's shop." They describe the tortures that lie ahead should he stay. Of Turandot, they say, "What is she? A female with a crown on her head, if you strip her naked she's flesh, raw flesh, inedible stuff." They warn him to keep clear of Turandot's riddles, but Calaf refuses to listen. The ministers then try another approach: "Turandot doesn't exist. There exists only the Nothingness in which you annihilate yourself." All is illusion, they insist – neither Turandot nor Calaf, god nor man, exists.

Calaf pushes them aside and runs to the gong just as the executioner appears on the ramparts with the severed head of the Prince of Persia. Timur pleads one last time with his son – as does Liù, in her beautiful aria "Signore, ascolta" (Sir, listen), another melody based on a traditional Chinese tune. She tells Calaf she can stand no more. She has come so far with his name on her lips, but if his fate is sealed the next day, she and Timur will die on the road of exile. "Timur will lose his son, I, the shadow of a smile." Calaf turns to the sobbing girl and tries to comfort her: "Non piangere, Liù" (Don't cry, Liù).

In the sextet that follows, Liù and Timur plead with Calaf, who asks their forgiveness but sees only "Her radiant face, she calls me! I follow my destiny." Ping, Pang, and Pong repeat "Death, death, death" as the crowd intones, "We are digging a grave for you who challenges love." At last, Calaf runs to the great gong and strikes it three times. "Turandot!" he calls. Her theme thunders forth from the orchestra as the curtain falls.

Act II opens on the next day, the day of the trial. Here, Puccini gives us a brief respite from the high drama of Act I: in the broad light of day, Ping, Pang, and Pong discuss the state of affairs in China. The baritone Ping, leader of the trio, and the tenors, Pang and Pong, recall the past: "O China, how happily you slept for seventy thousand centuries when everything went according to the ancient rule, and then was born Turandot." They add up the number of beheadings from past years, discuss the young men who "lose their heads" over a powerful and beautiful idol who has no interest in them, and wonder if they will be preparing a wedding or a funeral for the Unknown Prince.

The sounds of drums, trumpets, and trombones call

them back to reality. It is time to go to the trial. There follows a magnificent march based on pentatonic Chinese motifs as the crowd assembles around a huge, central staircase: servants bearing brightly colored lanterns precede the mandarins in brilliant costumes, followed by the eight sages with the scrolls bearing the answers to Turandot's riddles. Ping, Pang, and Pong enter and take their places. Incense rises as, last of all, at the highest level, the old Emperor appears to the music of China's imperial anthem. The Unknown Prince stands at the foot of the stairs; Timur and Liù are among the crowd.

In a slow, faint voice, unaccompanied by the orchestra, the frail Emperor tells the Unknown Prince that a terrible oath binds him to his promise to Turandot, and offers the Prince a last chance to leave. Calaf's answer is quiet but firm: He will face the trial. The Emperor sighs, "So be it. Let your destiny be fulfilled." The Mandarin reads again the terms of the decree, and Turandot appears, magnificently attired. Cold, regal, and impassive, she looks indifferently at the Prince, who returns her gaze with ardent determination. She address Calaf in the great, technically grueling aria "In questa reggia:" "In this palace, thousands of years ago, a desperate cry rang out, a cry that took refuge in my soul. Princess Lo-u-Ling, my ancestress, sweet and serene, one night was dragged away into the atrocious night where her fresh voice was extinguished." Now Princes come from every part of the world to try their fate, but Turandot wants only revenge for Lo-u-Ling's cry and her death. Turandot has no idea that the prince standing before her is the son of Timur, a descendent of the Tartar king who destroyed her ancestress. "No one will ever possess me. Stranger, don't tempt fate. The riddles are three, death is one." The aroused Prince throws Turandot's challenge back at her, singing the same melody but higher up the scale: "No, no, the riddles are three, one is life." The two repeat these lines together at ever higher pitches until the trumpets announce the beginning of the trial.

Poised and confident, Turandot poses the first riddle: "What is it that is born each night, only to die the next day?" Calaf responds at once: "Hope!" The sages unfold their scrolls, read, and nod in agreement. Turandot, surprised, descends a few steps toward Calaf, who kneels before her. Accompanied by nervous strings and timpani beats, she asks the second riddle: "What is like a flame yet is not a flame, it grows cold when life is lost and burns when life is won?" Calaf hesitates a moment, then answers: "Blood!" Again he is right. Turandot descends the last few steps to Calaf and looks fiercely into his eyes: "What is the frost that sets you aflame? If it wants you free, it enslaves you; if it takes you for slave, you are king." Calaf pauses a long time in agonizing silence; then, as if inspired, he leaps to his feet and cries out, "Turandot!"

The Princess steps back, appalled. The impossible has happened – he has answered all three riddles correctly, and she has lost. She turns to the Emperor and implores him not to cast his daughter into the arms of this stranger. The Emperor insists the oath is sacred and that she must abide by its terms. Turandot furiously forbids the Unknown Prince to look at her. "No one will ever possess me! Do you want to take me by force?" Calaf, ecstatic and victorious, cries, "No, I want you ardent with love!" He suggests a solution: In exchange for her three riddles, he will ask but one of her: If she can discover his name before dawn, he will die; if she cannot, she will be his. Turandot nods imperiously and leaves as the entire cast sings the imperial anthem.

Like the first, the third and final act is set at night. To haunting music, voices sing in the distance: "Thus commands Turandot, let no one sleep this night in Peking." Echoing voices sing a lament, "Nessun dorma" (None shall sleep). The Unknown Prince, sitting on the steps of a pavilion, picks up the soft refrain and sings a beautiful *romanza*. "None shall sleep! You too, princess, are sitting in your cold room gazing at the stars. My mystery is locked in me, no one shall know my name." The quiet mood is broken by Ping, Pang, and Pong, fearful that if the Prince's name is not discovered, they will suffer. They tempt Calaf with beautiful women, treasure, and glory, but he does not yield.

Suddenly, guards appear dragging Timur and Liù, bloodstained and beaten. "They know the name!" Ping cries out. Turandot arrives, and Ping assures her they will force the secret from the old man and the girl by torture. The Unknown Prince tries to intervene. "They don't know me," he insists. "We'll see," Turandot grimly replies. The guards seize Timur, but before they can hurt him, Liù runs forward. "Only I know his name – but I will keep his secret." Infuriated, Turandot orders that Liù be tortured. When her suffering becomes unbearable, Turandot advances toward the girl and demands, almost in spite of herself, "Who placed such strength in your heart?" "Love," Liù gasps. "Love so great that these sufferings are sweet because I offer them to my Lord. I give him to you, Princess, and I lose all." Turandot orders the torture to continue. Liù speaks one last time: "You who are girded with frost, overcome by such flame, you also will love him." With that, the desperate girl grabs a dagger from one of the guards and plunges it into her heart.

Liù's suicide horrifies the crowd. "My little Liù," Calaf mourns, as Turandot seizes a whip from the guard whose dagger Liù used and lashes the guard in the face. Timur, unaware that Liù is dead, reaches for her, begging her to rise and open her eyes. His despair is pitiable, and the crowd fears that Liù's "offended spirit will avenge itself" on them. Turandot's servants cover her face with a white veil. Liù's body is lifted and carried off, Timur walking at her side, holding her hand. "Liù, let us walk together one more time. I'll follow you into the night that has no morning." The keening crowd follows the funeral procession off into the darkness.

Here was where Puccini finished composing, unable to

complete the opera.

Calaf and Turandot are left alone on stage. She, motionless behind her white veil, stands before an infuriated Calaf. "Lift that veil and see the purest blood that was shed for you," he commands and tears the veil from her face, as she rigidly accuses him of sacrilege: "I am no human, I am a daughter of heaven." Calaf stands for a moment, as if bewitched – then says, "Your soul is on high, but your body is near." With that he embraces her and kisses her passionately on the mouth. Turandot attempts to resist, but then capitulates – she has no more voice, no more strength, no more will. Like Sleeping Beauty and Brünnhilde before her, she is transformed by the Prince's kiss. "What has become of me?" she murmurs as her eyes fill with tears.

Calaf responds with infinite tenderness, but Turandot looks beyond him at the sky. "It is dawn. Turandot's sun is setting. My glory has ended." She sings a beautiful aria, "Del primo pianto" (Of the first weeping), in which she tells the prince that, from the first time she saw him, she feared for him, "There was in your eyes the light of heroes. I hated you for that, and for that I loved you. I was torn between two terrors, to conquer you or to be conquered. But now I am conquered by this fire, terrible and sweet." She asks that he leave the court, his mystery unrevealed. But Calaf, sure of her now, responds impetuously, "I will give you my name and my life: I am Calaf, son of Timur." For a wild moment, Turandot's vengeful spirit returns. "I know your name," she gloats. "I am mistress of your life, your fate. It is mine." The intoxicated Calaf responds joyously, "Take it, then. Death is beautiful!"

Turandot at once understands that he has given his life into her hands. But now that she knows his name, things change: She can no longer see him as a vague, painful memory of a distant past, but must face and accept him as a unique individual. Regally, she commands, "Calaf, stand before the people with me." Trumpets blare, full daylight floods the stage, and the Emperor waits on high for his daughter. "August father, I know the name of the stranger." Turandot looks at Calaf and says softly, almost to herself, "His name is . . . Love." Calaf breathes an enormous sigh of relief and embraces her as the crowd goes wild, throwing flowers, exulting in the happy ending as the heroic couple sing "Love, Eternal Love" to a thunderous reprise of – not Turandot's theme, as one might expect, but Calaf's "Nessun dorma."

So ends the fairytale. But once we recover from the beauty, excitement, and drama of Puccini's music – for *Turandot* is opera at its extravaganza best – the questions remain. How is Turandot transformed from a cruel, icy princess to a loving, warm-blooded human being? How is Calaf so blinded by passion that he can observe – in fact, be the cause of – Liù's death, then, moments later, kiss her murderess? Had Puccini lived to finish the opera, to supervise its premiere and make revisions, we might have had answers to these questions. Perhaps, had the composer been able to find that transcendent place in which the princess is transformed from passive prize into a willing participant in a relationship of free, loving, and unselfish commitment, then Turandot and Calaf might have been transfigured into godlike status.

Turandot is an enigma. She causes Liù's suffering and witnesses her pain, and even asks Liù what it is that gives her such strength. Liù's simple answer, "Love," takes Turandot aback. This was something she had not considered. Love? How could that be? Puccini, in creating Liù, said, "I believe that Liù must sacrifice herself because of some sorrow, but I don't see how this can be developed unless we make her die under torture. And why not? Her death could be an element in softening the heart of the princess."

What was the turning point for Turandot? When Calaf answers the riddles, she fully expects him to carry her off by force, as happened to her ancestress. But he knows another way, the mere possibility of which is alien to her. He wants her "ardent with love and burning with passion." He so much wants her to come to him of her own free will that he is prepared to sacrifice himself. Unsure of how to proceed in the face of such an unexpected turn of events, Turandot hesitates. Until the opera's final moments, no one can be sure that she will not revert to her old vindictive self and destroy Calaf. This is the dramatic masterstroke that keeps listeners on the edges of their seats until the very end of the opera.

As it stands, the opera suggests that, as in fairytale or myth, it is the kiss of the prince that awakens the princess to love. Puccini was a passionate man who equated love and sex with guilt; as the creator of the heroines he loved so deeply, he also had the power to make them pay for the sin of loving. With Turandot, it was to be different. Calaf's kiss, beyond being a purely sensual experience, awakens Turandot from her prison of misplaced terror and childhood fears, as represented by the story of Lo-u-Ling, to a true maturity in which she can leave the past behind and no longer feel threatened.

The great soprano Johanna Meier said of this challenging role, "To give this opera its true depth, Turandot must be able to soar through those incredible phrases, and then melt convincingly into utter femininity at the end. One must look beyond the icy, imperious character to the frightened and vulnerable woman beneath the façade."

Calaf is another enigma: in his heartless lack of concern for Liù, to whom he clearly owes an enormous debt for her caring for his father, and in his abandonment of both his long-lost father and Liù the minute he falls in love with the image of Turandot. Calaf stands by and watches Liù tortured when he could easily end her suffering by revealing his name. Then, amazingly, after witnessing Liù's death, he instantly forgets her, hypnotized by Turandot. Despite being appalled by the princess's cruelty, his only thought is to tear off her veil and kiss her. Like his creator, Puccini, Calaf is aroused by pain and suffering. While composing *Turandot*, Puccini went so far as to admit that "I have the great weakness of being able to compose only when my puppet executioners come on the stage." Fr. Owen Lee suggests, "His creative powers quickened when he had before him a specimen of human suffering." Not even in *Tosca* did Puccini portray suffering and torture so graphically as in *Turandot*; at least in *Tosca*, Cavaradossi is tortured offstage; Liù is made to suffer center stage, in the limelight.

The other side of Calaf's nature is that of a generous, even noble man. Having won Turandot, he offers her a way out by proposing a riddle for her. He trusts her with his life, believing his love to be invincible. Convinced that Turandot is his destiny, he is single-minded in his pursuit of her. But while Calaf was sure of his destiny, Puccini could only reach for the stars with his very genuine talent, plagued as he was by chronic self-doubt. Calaf, the most heroic of all of Puccini's male characters, is possibly the one character that Puccini would have most liked to become.

Puccini invented the character of Liù; she does not exist in Gozzi's tale. Puccini knew about the suffering of love from the sad sexual escapades of his own life. He never forgot the suicide of Doria Manfredi, his maid servant, which happened during the composition of *Madama Butterfly*. Manfredi's innocent affection for Puccini caused Elvira, Puccini's wife, to be so jealous and vindictive that Doria poisoned herself. Shades of Manfredi can be found in the innocent, helpless love of the servant girl for her master. Liù's devotion to the man she loves also recalls the suffering heroines who preceded her – the little Madama Butterfly, the tubercular Mimi, the outcast Manon. Liù even echoes Anna in *Le Villi*, Puccini's first opera – and the only other one he based on a fairytale – in which Anna, rejected by her lover, haunts him in death. Liù is sister to Lo-u-Ling,

Turandot's murdered ancestress, whom Turandot describes as "sweet and serene." In psychological terms, Liù represents a mother figure who is eternally young, but who must be removed before Calaf/Puccini can move forward to a mature, unselfish relationship. The romance of the idealized woman is what must die so that a mature relationship with the other, (who is always merely another flawed human being), can be born.

At Liù's death, Puccini laid down his pen, able to conceive of such a relationship intellectually but unable to express in music what he himself had not experienced. Still, the opera he left us with can be seen as an appeal to overcome feelings of fear and pride, to relinquish the desire for conquest and domination in order to achieve an ideal relationship.

"Chi ha vissuto per amore, per amore si mori" (He who lives for love dies for love), sings the Street-Song vendor in Puccini's *Il Tabarro*. Puccini believed this theme, and so his suffering heroines had to die. In *Turandot*, however, he wanted to go beyond this, to describe a union in which a man and woman join together in perfect harmony with no expectations or demands on either side. Rather than fulfilling the tradition of the fairytale Prince who takes his winnings, his bride (whether she likes it or not), half the kingdom, and walks happily off into a bright new day, Calaf freely offers his life to Turandot. Knowing that there is a real possibility that she will destroy him, he gives himself into her power. He does this not once but twice after he has "won" her. Calaf's unselfish actions open Turandot's eyes to the possibility of love on an equal basis which allows her to descend from her icy isolation to freely accept his love.

Because Puccini had never experienced such love, the ending of *Turandot* presented a problem to him. He wanted *Turandot* to end with a love duet of the stature of *Tristan und Isolde* ("Then Tristan" was marked in Puccini's jottings on the unfinished score), but Puccini did not have Wagner's unique genius – or, for that matter, Mozart's extraordinary compassion. With either, he might have brought *Turandot* to the transcendent, potentially mythic conclusion he envisioned. In September 1924, two months before his death, he wrote, "It must be a great duet. These two almost superhuman beings descend through love to the level of mankind, and this love must at the end take possession of the whole stage in a great orchestral peroration."

Turandot is both a fairytale and a *verismo* opera, (a true-to-life approach in dealing with reality). It focuses on death: the death of the suitors, whose disembodied heads line the ramparts of the palace; the beheading of the Prince of Persia; the constant threat of death for Timur and Calaf; and, above all, the cruel onstage death of Liù. Puccini may even have had a premonition of his own death at the time of composition. He said, in his last months, "The opera will be given incomplete, and someone will come to the front and say, 'At this point the Master died.'" Near the end of *Turandot*, Calaf cries out, "Death is beautiful." Though only 64, Puccini had perhaps by then had enough of life's struggles and, like his hero, welcomed death.

Death came for Puccini two months after he composed the death of Liù. In the late summer of 1924 he became increasingly ill, his voice hoarse and painful with a persistent cough. The old doubts returned that had plagued him throughout his career – that he lacked the ability to achieve the greatness he sought. He traveled with his son, Tonio, for treatment in Brussels, where he endured a painful surgical procedure in which radioactive needles were placed in the cancerous growth in his throat. He survived the surgery, but five days later his heart failed, and he died on November 24.

It was now up to another composer to complete *Turandot*. Arturo Toscanini, Puccini's close friend and colleague – and who 30 years before had conducted Puccini's first opera, the fairytale *Le Villi* – took on the task of seeing *Turandot* finished. He assigned a young composer, Franco Alfano, the job of using Puccini's notes and sketches to finish the opera.

Alfano remained faithful to Puccini, showing, one critic said, "Extreme respect and loyalty to Puccini's intentions." The collaboration between Toscanini and Alfano was, however, difficult, and the rehearsals were stormy. At first, Toscanini wanted the ending expanded, then rejected Alfano's attempts to do so. As performed today, the great duet and finale are effective and do indeed provide catharsis and closure, albeit without Puccini's genius and inspiration.

The eagerly anticipated premiere of *Turandot* at La Scala, on April 26, 1926, was an resounding success. As he had promised Puccini, Toscanini conducted. At the death of Liù, Toscanini laid down his baton, turned to face the audience, and said, "Here ends the opera left incomplete by the Maestro, who died at this point." The following evening, the completed opera, with Alfano's ending, was presented for the first time.

♪

Characters

Princess Turandot	soprano
Emperor Altoum	tenor
Timur, exiled king of Tartary	bass
Calaf, his son, the Unknown Prince	tenor
Liù, a slave girl	soprano
Ping, Grand Chancellor	baritone
Pang, Grand Purveyor	tenor
Pong, Chief Cook	tenor

Bibliography

Carner, Mosco. *Puccini*. New York: Alfred A. Knopf, 1959.

Heuscher, Julius. *Psychology, Folklore, Creativity and the Human Dilemma*. Springfield, IL: Charles C. Thomas, 2003. Also: personal communications with the author.

John, Nicholas. *Turandot*, English National Opera Guide 27. New York: Riverrun Press, 1984.

Lee, Owen. *First Intermissions*. Oxford University Press, 1995.

Newman, Ernest. *Great Operas, Vol. II*. New York: Vintage Books, 1959.

Osborne, Charles, *The Complete Operas of Puccini*. New York: Da Capo Press, 1981.

Peter Grimes

Benjamin Britten

*P*eter Grimes is the creation of Benjamin Britten (1913–1976), England's finest composer of opera in the 20th century. In this work, Britten wrote of what he knew and loved: the cold, blustery, windswept coast of East Anglia; the dark, living sea; and the people who inhabit the seaside towns along its shores. The opera is the tragedy of a loner ostracized by his society while yearning to be part of it, an aggressive fisherman who is not prepared to suffer slander or people who whisper behind his back. The violent Grimes is a proud visionary with a dream that can never be realized in The Borough, where he was born, a place he cannot leave because, as he explains, "I am native, rooted here … By familiar fields, marsh and sand, ordinary streets, prevailing wind." The opera is a haunting work like no other.

The Borough was the 18th-century name of a small fishing village on the east coast of England. Over time, the name evolved into Olde Borough, and eventually into Aldeburgh, the name by which it is known today. Since 1948, the year of the first Aldeburgh Festival, the town has become internationally famous for its summer music festival, which Britten founded. It was here that the composer lived, wrote, found his characters, and presented his operas.

Nearly two centuries earlier, George Crabbe (1754–1832), a clergyman and poet who had been born in Aldeburgh, wrote a long narrative poem in rhyming couplets, *The Borough* (1810), about the place and its inhabitants, in which he depicted the harsh reality of a community at the mercy of the winds and the North Sea tides as it struggled to make a living from the sea. Crabbe described the bigotry and hypocrisy of the villagers, who defend themselves at any cost against those who do not conform to their ways – men such as Peter Grimes. Fearful of what they do not understand, the villagers malign, hunt down, and ultimately destroy those whom they perceive to be threats to their own tenuous survival. In one section of the poem, "The Poor of the Borough," Grimes is described as a vicious, cruel, heartless man who takes child apprentices to help him on his fishing boat. He sadistically mistreats the boys, wreaking his personal angst and torment on the defenseless youngsters; by the start of the poem, two boys have already died in his care. Rejected by the community for the boys' deaths and haunted by visions of his own dead father, who appears to him leading two ghostly apprentices by the hand, Grimes goes mad. Crabbe's Grimes is a man "untouched by pity, unstung by remorse, and uncorrected by shame; yet is this hardihood of temper and spirit broken by want, disease, solitude and disappointment; and he becomes the victim of a horror-stricken fantasy" (from Crabbe's Preface to *The Borough*). The character of Grimes was based on a violent fisherman, Tom Brown, who lived in Aldeburgh in the mid-18th century and who, it was rumored, had caused the deaths of his boy apprentices.

In an article about Crabbe's poetry published in *The Listener* in 1941, E. M. Forster described Aldeburgh as "a bleak little place: not beautiful. It huddles around a flint-towered church and sprawls down to the North Sea – and what a wallop the sea makes as it pounds at the shingle. Nearby is a quay, at the side of an estuary, and here the scenery becomes melancholy and flat; expanses of mud, saltish commons, the marsh birds crying." Benjamin Britten, reading this article in San Diego, California, where he then lived, said that it recalled vividly "the realities of that grim and exciting sea coast around Aldeburgh." He reported later that, on finding a copy of Crabbe's poem in a bookstore in Los Angeles, "I suddenly realized where I belonged and what I lacked. I had become without roots." Intrigued by the poem and homesick for England, Britten and his life-long partner, the tenor Peter Pears (1910–1986), decided to return home and use *The Borough* as the source of an opera, to be called *Peter Grimes*.

Pacifists and conscientious objectors, Britten and Pears had left England in 1939, at the beginning of World War II, and their departure was viewed unfavorably by the British public. They lived in New York, where Britten composed his first opera, on the unlikely American folk tale of Paul Bunyan, with a libretto by another British expatriate, W. H. Auden. *Paul Bunyan* was not a success, and they moved to California. On the ship back to Britain in 1942, Britten and Pears transformed Crabbe's poem into an outline for an opera. Later, Pears said, "By the time we came back to London, the whole story of *Peter Grimes* as set in the opera was already shaped." Britten invited poet and playwright Montagu Slater, for whom he had earlier composed incidental music, to provide the libretto. The collaboration, which continued over two years, proved to be difficult. Britten was never satisfied with Slater's depiction of Grimes and made numerous changes, insisting that the fisherman be portrayed as an introverted man isolated by his community instead of the cruel, vicious man in Crabbe's poem.

In Britten's version of Crabbe's story, Grimes is a

multidimensional character whose ruthlessness is offset by suffering, guilt, and wounded pride – an idealist with a quick temper, a man both violent and vulnerable. Pears described Grimes as "Clumsily violent, but not a sadist at all. I see him as an oversensitive being: too unstable, too strong in his reactions, too unsure of his reactions." Britten and Pears clearly identified with the lonely fisherman in his fight against a closed and unforgiving community. Grimes, in their view, becomes the symbol of the artist standing at the edge of his society, a symbol for the two men of their personal situation and their less than total acceptance by British society because of their suspected relationship (at the time, homosexuality was still illegal in England) and their status as conscientious objectors. Britten said, "A certain feeling for us was that of the individual against the crowd, with ironic overtones for [Britten and Pears's] own situation. As conscientious objectors we were out of it [and] we experienced tremendous tension. I think it was partly this feeling which led us to make Grimes a character of vision and conflict, rather than the villain he was in Crabbe."

Britten composed *Peter Grimes* in Aldeburgh from 1943 to 1945; the premiere was presented at war's end, in June 1945, by the Sadler's Wells Opera Company in London, with Peter Pears, who had played such a large part in the opera's creation, in the title role. The opera was received enthusiastically, is now accepted as a landmark work in the genre of modern English opera, and cemented Britten's and Pears's attachment to East Anglia, where they lived and worked for the rest of their lives.

Different singers approach the role of Grimes very differently. Pears interpreted the role sympathetically, almost poetically; Jon Vickers, another celebrated Grimes, firmly expressed the character's deep-seated anger from his very first entrance, laying bare the agony of the outsider with an emotional nakedness and a high dramatic intensity that were unforgettable. Vickers said of the role, "Peter

Grimes is a study in the entire human psychology of human rejection." Johanna Meier, the soprano who sang the role of Ellen Orford opposite Vickers, said, "Grimes must be played by a superb singing actor since so much of the opera is subtle and mood-oriented. Vickers's personality was ideal for the role. ... tormented, angry, yet to be pitied." Tenor Philip Langridge gives Grimes an intelligence that brings out the man's tortured longing, his harshness and cruelty to the boy apprentice, and his love/hate relationship with Ellen. His disintegration into madness is entirely real and believable. (Both Vickers's and Langridge's performances of *Peter Grimes* are available on DVD.) To varying degrees, all three singers raise questions central to the opera: Is Grimes to be pitied or blamed? Is he a victim or is he guilty?

The opera opens with a Prologue, which depicts the inquest in which Grimes is interrogated about the death of his apprentice at sea. The truculent Grimes takes the oath from the witness box, surrounded by the villagers, most of whom have already decided that he is guilty. For the inhabitants of this small, insular village, no rumor is too small to be overlooked and amplified. Grimes describes how he had caught a catch too big to sell in the Borough and so, with the boy, set sail for London. The boat was blown off course and for three days they were at the mercy of the sea. They ran out of drinking water, and the boy grew weaker and weaker and "died there amongst the fish." Grimes threw the catch overboard and returned to home port with the boy's body.

Britten uses an original technique in the Prologue to introduce the villagers, bringing them forward one by one from the crowd as the magistrate states their names. (Wagner did a very similar thing in Act I, Sc. iii of *Meistersinger*, when Fritz Kothner calls the roll for the Mastersingers' meeting). We meet the pompous Swallow, the magistrate who leads the proceedings; Ellen Orford, the widowed schoolmistress; Ned Keene, the apothecary and quack, who is the least biased against Grimes; the rector, Mr. Horace Adams, who, locked into narrow dogma, is unable to take a stand one way or another; the widow, Mrs. Sedley, a vicious gossip, self-assertive and unpopular, who lives from one dose of laudanum to the next; Auntie,* the lively landlady of The Boar, the pub where people meet, drink, and flirt with her two pretty "Nieces" – girls of easy virtue who are The Boar's main attraction; Bob Boles, the rabble-rousing evangelical Methodist; and Hobson, the mail carrier, who is also the constable.

These characters make up the village, each carefully characterized by Britten in the score, and united in their dislike of Grimes. Colin Graham, a noted director of many *Grimes* productions who worked closely with Britten and Pears at Aldeburgh, said, "I know of no other opera where the chorus has such an enormous responsibility, where it carries a significance equal to that of the principals. In fact, the majority of the soloists are only the mouthpieces of different sections of the community."

When the magistrate, Swallow, rules that, given the evidence, the boy's death was accidental, the crowd grumbles at the verdict. He forbids Grimes to take another apprentice unless he "Can get a woman to help you look after him." Grimes states that he must have a boy to help with his boat, as to a woman, "That's what I want – but not yet – not till I've stopped people's mouths." Swallow clears the court and the villagers leave. Only Ellen Orford, the widowed schoolmistress, remains to ask the rough fisherman to "come away," but Grimes, angry at the town and its gossip, is focused on the past and cannot see beyond it. Their duet begins bitonally, he in F minor, she in E major, but by the end they sing in unison, two lonely souls reaching out to one another, unable to find common ground.

Act I begins, as does each act of this opera, with an exquisite prelude. This first one, titled *Dawn*, paints a

---

* "Auntie" in the early 19th century could mean procuress.

picture of waves lapping on the shore, sea birds crying, and the sea itself in constant motion as strings, flutes, and woodwinds gently describe the early-morning tide. As the fishermen return home with their catch, their women leave off mending the nets to take in the big baskets of fish; some of the men drift into the pub, where Auntie greets them. Balstrode, a retired sea captain, calmly watches the town's daily goings-on and notices an ominous storm building at sea. "The wind is holding back the tide. If the wind veers around, watch for your lives," he warns. Peter Grimes is heard offstage, calling for help with his boat; all turn their backs on him but Balstrode and Ned Keene, who turn the capstan to pull the boat in to shore as Boles shouts derisively at them, "This lost soul of a fisherman must be shunned by society."

When the boat is secured, Keene tells Grimes that he has found him another "workhouse brat" to serve as Grimes's apprentice. In mid-19th-century England, orphaned children with no family or means of support were taken in by the church or state and raised, typically, in appalling conditions. A tradesman who needed an apprentice could legally buy an orphan from the workhouse to help him at his trade; Grimes's first apprentice had come to him this way. But when Boles asks, "Is this a Christian country? Are pauper children so enslaved that their bodies go for cash?" no one listens – the community turns blind eyes and deaf ears to these children's fate. Hobson, instructed to collect the boy and deliver him to Grimes, clearly doesn't want the task. He demurs, until Ellen Orford steps forward and offers to go with him to accompany the child. The crowd is scornful of her gesture of kindness, "You'll be Grimes's messenger" but Ellen stands her ground. "Let her among you without fault cast the first stone," she reminds them as she follows Hobson out. Mrs. Sedley takes Keene aside to ask when her laudanum will be in. "Tonight," he replies, "When Hobson returns." Balstrode calls out, "The spring tide is here with a gale behind," and the villagers head for the shelter and warmth of The Boar.

Balstrode remains outside a few moments to talk with Grimes. He suggests to the troubled man that he leave the village and try "the wider sea," but Grimes is determined to stay. "I am native, rooted here." He will not leave even when he learns that the mothers of the village terrify their misbehaving children by telling them, "You'll be sold to Peter Grimes." Balstrode rationalizes, "Your boy was workhouse starved, maybe that's why he died." Grimes relives the boy's death, then, as the storm builds, defiantly tells Balstrode of his dream. "I have my visions, I know a way to answer the Borough, I'll win them over. They listen to money. I'll fish the sea dry, set up household and shop and marry Ellen." Balstrode encourages him to "Go and ask her, without your booty, she'll have you now." But Grimes will not have Ellen marry him out of pity. The men argue. "Are you my conscience?" Grimes asks angrily. Balstrode shrugs his shoulders and goes into The Boar. Left alone, Grimes cries to the heavens – "What harbor shelters peace?" He thinks of Ellen and longs for the peace he will find in the harbor of her arms.

As Grimes lumbers off into the night, the *Storm* interlude describes the wild fury of the wind, gusts of spray blowing across the tops of the white-crested waves. In George Crabbe's words, the waves

> *Curled as they come, they strike with furious force*
> *And then re-flowing, take their grating course,*
> *Raking the rounded Flints, which ages past*
> *Roll's by their rage, and shall to ages last.*

The scene and music shift from the wild exterior of the stormy seafront to the interior of The Boar. The Nieces run downstairs, frightened – the wind has blown their windows in. When Balstrode pokes fun at their fear, Auntie reprimands him: "A joke's a joke and fun is fun, but say your grace and be polite for all we've done." The drunken Boles makes a pass at the girls and gets into a fight with Balstrode, who subdues him, singing, "We live and let live and look, we keep our hands to ourselves." Ned Keene runs in to tell the crowd that the cliff behind Grimes's hut has been washed away. The tension builds as reports of the worsening storm reach the village. Then the door bursts open and Grimes appears, wild and exhilarated by the storm. The crowd mutters that he is the devil waiting for his apprentice. Grimes ignores them and sings an exultant aria, "Now the Great Bear and Pleiades," in which his reaching high notes, sung at full voice at the height of a storm in a pub before dumbstruck villagers, make this aria one of the opera's most memorable moments. Most of the words are pitched on the same note E, an effect which Britten said, "crystallizes and holds the emotion of a dramatic situation." The aria ends with the desperate question, "Who can turn skies back and begin again?"

The villagers think Grimes is drunk – "His song alone would sour the beer." Their growing anger and Grimes's defiance accelerate until Balstrode intervenes. "For peace's sake, someone start a song," he says, and the round "Old Joe has gone fishing" gets underway. Caught up in the song's complex rhythms, the crowd momentarily forgets Grimes, until he breaks in with verses of his own in his own rhythm and spoils the fun. Again the pub door bursts open, this time revealing Ellen, Hobson, and the boy, John, all soaked to the skin. Auntie offers brandy and hot water, but Grimes rudely pushes his way forward and insists that the boy leave with him at once. Ellen has no choice but to give the boy up, and Grimes heads out into the night, pushing the frightened boy before him.

Another interlude, a lovely tone poem, "Sunday Morning," opens Act II, shifting the mood away from the anger of the storm toward one of peace and calm. Church bells can be heard calling the villagers to prayer. Ellen, who decides not to attend the service on this bright, sunny day, sings of the

"Glitter of waves and glitter of sunlight," as gentle phrases from the horns and sparkling woodwinds describe the day. The church service continues offstage throughout this scene as, onstage, Ellen talks first with the boy, then with Grimes. The boy looks nervous and has little to say. Ellen sings of her love of children then stops when she notices a tear in the boy's coat. He tries to pull away from her, but she insists that he let her see, and discovers a huge bruise on his neck. She is shocked and hurt. "Well, it's begun." She tells the boy that this day, the Sabbath, will be a day of peace, but just then Grimes enters and calls the boy away. Ellen reminds him that it is Sunday, a day of rest, but Grimes violently insists, "This is whatever day I say it is. He works for me. Leave him alone. He's mine." Ellen asks about the bruise, then wonders aloud if they did the right thing in taking the boy from the orphanage. The infuriated Grimes shouts at her, "Wrong to plan? Wrong to try? Wrong to live?" At last, his temper gets the better of him and he strikes Ellen, then cries out in agony, "God have mercy on me." Grimes hurries off with the boy, leaving the devastated Ellen alone on stage. The villagers, who have been watching through the church's windows and half-closed doors, enter singing "Grimes is at his exercise," describing the fisherman's cruelty to the boy as, in the background, the church choir sings a benediction.

The service over, the villagers pour into the street and talk about what has happened. When Mrs. Sedley insists that Grimes is mistreating the boy, Balstrode cautions her against slander. Driven on by the phrase "Grimes is at his exercise," the crowd works itself up and turns on Ellen, accusing her of being Grimes's accomplice. She explains that she planned to care for the boy for Grimes, to mend his clothes and give him regular meals. Balstrode accuses the crowd of being "interfering gossips," but Swallow decides that the men will go to Grimes's hut to see what is going on; they storm offstage, chanting "Now is gossip put on trial." Ellen, Auntie, and the Nieces remain behind and sing a thoughtful quartet. Mindful of their plight, they sing philosophically of men, "From the gutter, why should we trouble at their ribaldries? Do we smile or do we weep, or wait quietly 'til they sleep?"

The interlude that takes us to Grimes's hut is a *Passacaglia* – a set of variations over an insistently repeated ground-bass theme in 4/4 time. The theme of "Grimes is at his exercise" is introduced in the bass with timpani beats, then taken up by a solo viola, Britten's instrument of choice to depict the voice of innocence. The variations describe the boy's sufferings, tears, fears, and pain.

Grimes's hut, built of an overturned boat, is sparsely but tidily furnished. There are two doors: one leads to the road, the other to a cliff, at the foot of which is moored Grimes's fishing boat. Grimes roughly orders the boy to dress in his sea boots, oilskin, sou'wester, and the sweater Ellen has knitted for him. Looking out over the cliff, Grimes sees the sea boiling with fish. He hurries the boy along, singing of Ellen, of his dreams for their future, and of his plan to buy respectability with the money he will earn – but the dream fades when he sees before him the ghost of the first apprentice. In the distance, the approaching crowd calls out Grimes's name. Grimes blames the boy for telling tales, then pushes the terrified lad toward the cliff-side door, insisting he go before him to the boat. The boy steps out, loses his footing, and screams as he falls down the ruined cliff into the sea. Grimes follows at once and disappears into the darkness as the angry crowd knocks on the front door. The men pour in to find everything quiet and shipshape, with no sign of Grimes or the boy. They look out over the collapsed cliff and estimate that it must be a 40-foot drop to the sea. Still finding no one about, the group leaves – all but Balstrode, who senses that all is not well. He goes to the cliff door, looks out, then climbs out to descend the cliff as the curtain falls.

Act III opens with a dance offstage in the village hall.

Swallow follows the Nieces onstage flirting with them to no avail. Mrs. Sedley tells Ned Keene that she is convinced that Grimes is a murderer, for no one has seen the boy for days. Ellen and Balstrode enter from the direction of the beach; Grimes's boat is in, but he has not been seen. Ellen has found the boy's jersey on the beach, the one she herself knitted, and knows what this means. Desperate in her feeling of powerlessness, she clings to the lost child's jersey as Balstrode tells her that Grimes now needs their help as never before. Mrs. Sedley, overhearing this conversation, goes to the villagers and insists they take action – the boy has been murdered. The people assemble, convinced more than ever of Grimes's guilt; now he must pay for his crimes, "Him who despises us, we'll destroy." The villagers scatter in all directions calling for vengeance.

The final interlude "Moonlight" suggests the crying of sea birds and the dark state of Grimes's mind. Beyond the ceaseless shifting motion of the sea a lone foghorn is heard in the distance. Clouds pass over the face of the moon to sustained chords, veils of aural mist like those that increasingly cloud Grimes's mind.

Grimes, a solitary figure by the side of his boat in the dark night, imagines that he is now going to a home "calm as deep water." Hearing the voices of the approaching crowd, he calls out to them, "Now is gossip put on trial? Land me. Turn the skies back and begin again." Now utterly alone in his madness, deserted by even the orchestra, Grimes sings a cappella. He reaches for Ellen's hand, but she is not there. To the chanting voices he cries, "To hell with your revenge. God have mercy on you." When Ellen and Balstrode appear, he is oblivious of their presence. Ellen tells him they have come to take him home. Balstrode tells the tormented man, "Come, I'll help you with your boat. Sail out 'til you lose sight of land. Then sink the boat. Good-bye, Grimes." The two men walk to the boat. Grimes climbs aboard, and Balstrode pushes it out into the water. Now, for the first time in this scene, the orchestra returns – a single violin plays the theme of the *Dawn* interlude, from the beginning of Act I. Balstrode waves farewell to Grimes, Ellen sobs, and Balstrode leads her quietly away.

As daylight fills the sky, the village wakens. Swallow reports that a boat has been sighted sinking out at sea, beyond reach. The villagers see nothing and turn back to the tasks of the day, forgetting the sinking boat, Grimes, and the dead boy. The outsider has gone from their midst; they close ranks and move on blindly with their lives to the opera's sad final chords.

This extraordinarily moving work has withstood the test of time. Britten brilliantly interweaves the six evocative Interludes, which describe the sea, Grimes's state of mind, and the changing moods of the community. (The Interludes are now frequently performed as concert excerpts under the title *Peter Grimes: Four Sea Interludes*.) Britten uses many traditional operatic forms to tell the tale: aria, recitative, duet, quartet, ensemble. Not so traditionally, entire sections are sung a cappella, and there is spoken dialogue – yet the work is through-composed, flowing without interruption from beginning to end. Much of the opera's greatness lies in Britten's orchestral colors and structural elements such as catchy tunes, right down to a sea shanty, which are balanced by soaring sections from Grimes and Ellen as each expresses his or her hopes and dreams. The folksy "Grimes is at his exercise" later becomes the poignant expression of the boy's pain in the *Passacaglia*, and is stated again in Grimes's desperate cry of "God have mercy on me." The music for the dance in The Boar becomes the music that drives the angry mob. In Britten's hands, seemingly simple melodies are made to express something much more profound.

The Borough's characters are vividly described in the music: the twittering, flirtatious Nieces have a whining theme in the storm scene, Mrs. Sedley sings "Murder most foul" in a dark minor key that says much about her drug-induced state, Swallow's music is fussy, Balstrode's is firm and resolute, and Auntie's "A joke's a joke" is jovial. The chorus's music shifts constantly and rhythmically, now sustained, now syncopated, driving the action irrevocably toward tragedy. Rare high notes from Ellen and Grimes rise above the voices of the malevolent, gossiping crowd and the brooding sea.

Dramatic scenes are highly charged by means of contrast: the juxtaposition of the offstage church service and the onstage argument between Grimes and Ellen suggests that Christian platitudes are given mere lip-service while truth and compassion are ignored by the congregation, who seek to destroy what they do not understand. Sudden shifts of mood are key components of the opera: the angry men's chorus contrasted with the calm quartet of the four women in Act II, the bouncy sea shanty interrupted by Grimes singing the same tune in a different rhythm, then Grimes's exultant aria, "Now the Great Bear and Pleiades" contrasted with the bickering of the villagers. A cappella sections sung against background chorus build tension at strategic moments in the action, most especially in the work's tragic conclusion.

In his notes for the first performance of *Peter Grimes*, Benjamin Britten said, "I wanted to express my awareness of the perpetual struggle of men and women whose livelihoods depend on the sea." At a later time he said, "It has to do with the people of the village." And finally, years later, "This is a subject very close to my heart – the struggle of the individual against the masses." His perception of the meaning and focus of the work changed over time.

In *Peter Grimes* many forces are at work: first and foremost is Grimes himself, the tortured soul who refuses to accept responsibility for the deaths of his apprentices yet who cannot live with his sense of guilt. The force of the sea underscores the action throughout, giving and taking, devouring Grimes's apprentices and finally claiming Grimes himself. And the blind, hypocritical community of the Borough feeds itself on gossip and destroys, as completely as does the sea, any who do not conform to its narrow way of life.

Characters

Peter Grimes, a fisherman	tenor
Ellen Orford, widow and schoolmistress	soprano
Balstrode, retired sea captain	baritone
Auntie, landlady of The Boar	contralto
Auntie's two Nieces	sopranos
Bob Boles, a fisherman and Methodist	tenor
Swallow, a lawyer and magistrate	bass
Mrs. Sedley, a widow	mezzo-soprano
Rev. Horace Adams, the rector	tenor
Ned Keene, apothecary	baritone
Hobson, the carrier	bass
John, the apprentice	silent role

Bibliography

Britten, Benjamin. *Peter Grimes*. Philip Langridge, Janice Cairns, others; David Atherton, cond.; English National Opera. DVD, Kultur D2902, 1995.

Britten, Benjamin. *Peter Grimes*. Jon Vickers, Heather Harper, others; Colin Davis, cond.; Royal Opera House, Covent Garden. DVD, Kultur D2255, 1981.

Goodwin, Noel. "Musical and Historical Note." *Peter Grimes* opera program. London: Royal Opera House Covent Garden, 1984.

Kennedy, Michael. *Britten*, Master Musicians series. Oxford University Press, 1993.

Lucas, F. L. *George Crabbe: An Anthology*. New York: Octagon Books, 1973.

Meier, Johanna. Personal communication, October, 2004.

Stearns, Maggie. "Peter Grimes: A Conversation with Colin Graham." Opera Theatre of St. Louis program, 1990.

Williams, Jeannie. *Jon Vickers: A Hero's Life*. Boston: Northeastern University Press, 1999.

The Barber of Seville

Gioacchino Rossini

Rosina sits in her room, embroidering and scheming. "I hate that old man," she says, stabbing her needle through the fabric. "Just as Lindoro was serenading me this morning, he had the nerve to come in and slam the window shut." She reflects, "Pity he caught me dropping that note. But I'll get even with him. He keeps me locked up in this house, I am bored to tears. I shall go crazy." She gets up and paces about the room. "I know what he wants. He wants to marry me and take my fortune. But I'll die before I marry that old bore, guardian or no. I have no one to talk to. Berta, the housekeeper, is always glum and moaning about the commotion in the house, and that slimy Don Basilio, who I'm sure is scheming with my guardian, gives me the creeps. Figaro is the only one I can talk to about the outside world. He was once manservant to the Count Almaviva, I hear." Rosina sits down before the locked balcony window that overlooks the courtyard below. "Lindoro sings so romantically. He may be a poor student, but I'm sure he will be a success. I wonder what he thought of my note? Maybe I'll write another and maybe Figaro can give it to him. Wait, here comes Figaro now!"

Thus the 16-year-old Rosina ruminates, plotting ways to escape the clutches of the elderly lawyer Dr. Bartolo, her guardian, with Figaro as her ally. In *The Barber of Seville*, she meets her match in Figaro. "I am the greatest," he informs one and all in his famous aria "Largo al factotum." Figaro serves everyone's needs and is in demand everywhere while being enormously popular and resourceful. In this he is like the men who gave him life: Pierre-Augustin Caron de Beaumarchais, who created him, and Gioacchino Rossini, who gave him immortality. The composite of these three men formed a life-force as recognizable, familiar, and amusing today as it was in 1755, when Figaro first appeared in Paris as the creation of Beaumarchais.

The famous overture to *Barber*, often played on its own as a concert piece, is a compilation of music Rossini composed for two earlier operas. (If an opera was not a success, he often culled the best numbers from it for use in later operas. For instance, part of the Count's final aria in *Barber* appeared a year later as one of the highlights of *La Cenerentola*, sung not by the tenor but the heroine.)

The story of this comedy of disguises and intrigue is hardly complicated. Rosina, the young ward of Dr. Bartolo, has just arrived home after a visit to Madrid, where she caught the eye of Count Almaviva, who has pursued her to Seville to further the relationship. On arriving, he discovers that Rosina is the virtual prisoner of her guardian, Dr. Bartolo, who is keeping her locked up in his house until he can marry her. The opera opens with the Count serenading Rosina under her window, accompanied by a group of paid musicians. Figaro, Almaviva's former servant, enters full of energy and life and the two men catch up on one another's news in a mood of light comedy and banter, paying little heed to the real reason they are there until Figaro finally reminds Almaviva that he had better get on with his serenade; he even loans the Count his guitar. The Count is not sure he can handle the guitar or the song, but Figaro/Rossini/Beaumarchais assure him that "when it comes to love-making, it doesn't matter if what one says makes sense or not," while reminding him that he cannot possibly sing a serenade in Seville without a guitar. The Count takes the guitar and sings at his servant's behest, telling Rosina that he is Lindoro, a poor student who loves her.

Figaro tells the Count that, as general factotum to the town, he has free access to the Bartolo household as "barber, surgeon, and apothecary," and devises a plan for the impatient Lindoro to meet Rosina: Lindoro will appear in the guise of a drunken soldier who is to be billeted at the house. Meanwhile, inside the house, Don Basilio, the conniving priest and singing master, arrives to inform Dr. Bartolo that Count Almaviva has been seen in town and is asking about Rosina. Bartolo determines then and there to wed his ward that very day. Basilio says he will spread a rumor around town about the Count "which will give him a bad odour as a man of evil reputation." Figaro later teases Rosina about her unknown suitor and suggests she write "Lindoro" a note; when she tells him it is already written, he laughs and fondly calls her a "crafty little schemer, who has found her match in me."

Loud knocking reveals a drunken soldier on the doorstep demanding admission. Rosina, peeking over the stairs, realizes at once it is Lindoro in disguise. Bartolo, furious at the intrusion, tries to have the noisy soldier thrown out and finally calls the police – but when Almaviva discreetly identifies himself, they refuse to arrest him. The whole cast is frozen in place ("Fredda ed immobile") by this amazing turn of events. The entire hilarious scene culminates in a thrilling crescendo as the curtain falls on Act I.

Almaviva/Lindoro's next disguise is as Don Alonzo, a young, enthusiastic priest who appears in Act II and informs

Dr. Bartolo that he has come in place of Don Basilio, who is very ill, to give Rosina her singing lesson. Believing that Alonzo is in collusion with Basilio in keeping the Count out of the way, Bartolo lets him in. In the middle of the singing lesson Figaro arrives to shave Bartolo; in the course of this broadly comic scene he manages to steal Bartolo's key to the balcony, which will enable the lovers to escape that night. During the singing lesson, whenever Bartolo is not looking, Lindoro and Rosina exchange sweet nothings and plan their escape. Then, just as things are moving along nicely, Don Basilio appears, miraculously recovered. Everyone is astonished, and the "sick" man is totally confused. Figaro, Lindoro, and Rosina manage (with the help of Lindoro's gold) to convince Basilio that he really is ill, and the rascally old priest is sent home to bed. Finally, Bartolo realizes that Alonzo is not what he seems and chases him out of the house. Left alone on stage, Berta, the old housekeeper, comments on love – "It's a tickling irritation, it's a torture, it's a passion" – as she wonders why there is always such chaos in the house.

But now night has fallen and a sudden summer storm is brewing in the beginnings of a magnificent Rossinian crescendo – lightning flashes from the flutes, tremolos rumble from the cellos, and pizzicato violins describe raindrops falling. A ladder appears at Rosina's window, and Figaro and Lindoro climb onto the balcony to find Rosina not willing but furious – Bartolo has convinced her that Lindoro was wooing her only on behalf of Count Almaviva. Amused, Lindoro throws off his disguise and tells Rosina he is none other than the Count himself. The delighted Rosina falls doubly in love (she is to marry the Count!), "Ah, quel colpo inaspettato" (Your romantic intimation) she sings joyfully, as Figaro urges the couple to leave quickly before Bartolo returns. Too late – the ladder has been taken from the window and they are trapped. Now Don Basilio arrives with a Notary, who is all prepared to marry Rosina to Bartolo. The quick-thinking Figaro steps forward and thanks the Notary for coming to marry Rosina to the Count. Bartolo arrives just after the deed is done and the marriage papers have been signed and sealed. The infuriated doctor is somewhat appeased when he learns that Almaviva plans to renounce Rosina's substantial dowry, which Bartolo would have had to pay, and the opera ends happily. Rossini leaves us laughing as Rosina gets her man, who happens to be the Count, and waltzes off with him to wedded bliss in one of the most beloved comic operas of all time.

The Barber of Seville does not require a lot of visual comedy, for a series of musical jokes is built into the score. The first words in Act I are "Piano, pianissimo," as Almaviva/Lindoro instructs his hired musicians to tiptoe about quietly so they will not waken anyone. When their exuberance at the size of their pay leads to a noisy crescendo of gratitude, Almaviva sends them away. Rossini repeats this ploy in the final trio, when Figaro urges the celebrating Rosina and Almaviva to be quiet and hurry lest their escape be discovered. Figaro imitates their love duet from the sidelines, echoing such words as "Rapture!" and "Forever!" Rossini's parody of long, extended duets undoes the couple – the escape ladder disappears and they are nearly caught. When Lindoro is warming to his topic in his serenade to Rosina, the window above is dramatically slammed shut, cutting him off in mid-verse – a musical slap in the face.

When Dr. Bartolo catches Rosina dropping a note to Lindoro over her balcony, she tells him that she's dropped the words of a new song, "The Useless Precaution," as Lindoro and Figaro stifle their laughter below. "It's the name of a new opera," she informs her suspicious guardian. Later, Bartolo gives his opinion of new operas: "An opera?" he grunts, "It will be the usual drama *semiserio*, a long, melancholy, boring, poetic farrago of nonsense. Barbarous taste. I can't stand this modern music." Rossini parodies himself, opera and Bartolo by having the venerable doctor sing in the old *semiserio* style during the singing lesson. The singing lesson itself is one long musical joke, as the lovers flirt with one another while pretending to be music teacher and student under the watchful eye of Bartolo, to the amusement of Figaro who, like the audience, knows exactly what is going on.

The opera's characters echo those found in the lively commedia dell'arte tradition: Figaro is the wily Harlequin; Rosina is Columbine, the clever, naughty, pretty, seductive young woman; the Count is the young lover; Don Basilio is the priest who is always there to be mocked; and Dr. Bartolo is a lawyer, always ripe for ridicule – in both play and opera, he is even called Dr. Baloardo (the commedia's name for this character). Beaumarchais describes Bartolo as "a stoutish, shortish, oldish, grayish, cunning, smarmy, posing, nosing, prying, peeping, creeping, whining, sniveling sort of man." Figaro describes the priest, Don Basilio, as a "matrimonial agent, a crooked fellow, a regular scoundrel, always short of money."

As with commedia characters, the young Almaviva wears a series of masks in the course of the opera, first presenting himself as the ardent Lindoro, a poor student who wants Rosina to love him for himself. Once in Bartolo's house, this time disguised as a drunken soldier, he cannot resist insulting the doctor, calling him Dr. Balordo, Bertoldo, Barbaro – this is pure commedia dell'arte. The "drunken" Count defends Rosina, and almost reveals his identity when he challenges Bartolo, who has threatened Rosina over the dropping of yet another love note (which she swears is only a laundry list). Almaviva's final disguise, dreamed up by Figaro, is as the young priest Don Alonzo, come in place of Don Basilio. In this guise he frustrates everyone with an interminably long greeting, "Pace e gioia" (Peace and joy), that is pure comedy – to the increasing annoyance of Bartolo, for even he must obey the rules of common courtesy.

Rosina role-plays from beginning to end. After all, what

is a shut-in, pent-up young woman to do but plot and plan ways to escape her wicked guardian? In her first cavatina (a short aria in one section), "Una voce poco fa" (The voice I just heard), she sings about herself. She has fallen in love with a song sung by Lindoro. She has not yet seen him, but she is desperate; he will be her means of escape. Rosina is not concerned with love – she just wants out. Displaying no symptoms of maidenly distress, Rosina spoils for a fight with all the eagerness of her teenage years, and with wild anticipation of the outcome. This challenging coloratura aria for a mezzo-soprano reveals a sharply etched portrait of a charming but vexing young woman. Rosina and Figaro revel in the challenges of the game. She cuts and thrusts with Bartolo, sharpening her wit and manipulative skills on him. In the singing lesson she keeps up the running joke about "The Useless Precaution" as she and Almaviva, who is now twice disguised as both Lindoro and Don Alonzo, sing the rondo "Love's a force there is no resisting, love will always triumph."

Rosina doesn't lose these personality traits when, years later, she is the Countess Almaviva in *The Marriage of Figaro*. Even in that opera, though her bright perkiness is somewhat subdued, she still plots and plans how to get back her once ardent, now philandering husband. She wins that battle also, again with Figaro's help, though Figaro by then is older, his wit intact but more cynical, and having some doubts about his own invincibility.

In *Barber*, Figaro's lively imagination drives the plot. Figaro is the puppet master and Almaviva, his puppet, dances on his strings. In Mozart's *The Marriage of Figaro*, Figaro actually sings "Se vuol balare" (I'll make him dance). Figaro's social criticism is not too barbed in the earlier opera; master and servant are united in the same cause – the abduction of Rosina. Figaro, with his many skills, loves the challenge of the deceit, to say nothing of his love of the gold the Count will give him if they succeed. The Count, for his part, needs Figaro's help if he is to win Rosina. Both men stand to gain: one intrigues for love, the other for money. This relationship changes in *The Marriage of Figaro* in which Figaro, resentful and critical of his master, is jealous of the overtures the Count makes toward Figaro's fiancée, Susanna. He spends his time in that opera, trying to outwit his master. In *Barber*, they are in cahoots.

One of the two bass roles, Dr. Bartolo, is the stock character in comic opera of the wicked guardian who plans to marry his young ward and take her fortune. Bartolo is unattractive but not stupid – when he sees ink stains on Rosina's fingers, he accuses her of writing a letter. Rosina wriggles out of this; she used a new pen, she says, to draw a flower on her embroidery. Both know the other is lying; the audience delights in being party to the deceits, and thrills to the scintillating volleys of words lobbed back and forth.

Bartolo plots with Basilio, but in the end is outwitted by everyone. In his Act I cavatina, "A un dottor della mia sorte" (For a doctor of my standing), he tells Rosina, "I must be treated with respect." She must beg his forgiveness for her bad behavior or be shut up "safely under lock and key." This aria starts out stuffy and smug; then, as Bartolo grows more agitated, the tempo quickens, and the whole piece wraps up with the lightning-fast *buffo* patter that is one of Rossini's trademarks. Rosina responds to all this under her singing breath: "If you want to sharpen the wits of a woman, all you need to do is turn the lock and key."

The opera's other bass is Don Basilio, the much caricatured and malingering priest who schemes with Bartolo but deserts him in the end. His most famous cavatina, and one of the best examples of Rossini's crescendo technique, is the "calumny aria." In "La Calunnia," a brilliant match of music to words, he describes how a rumor, once started, builds and builds until the victim of the rumor is "confounded and inexorably hounded out of society." Beaumarchais even used musical terms in this speech in his play: "*Pianissimo –*

a murmur and the poisoned seed is sown. Someone picks it up – *piano, piano*, and insinuates it into your ear. It spawns, creeps, spreads, multiplies and then – *rinforzando* – from mouth to mouth it goes like the very devil, and at last, like a thunderclap, becomes a crescendo." Rossini's Basilio takes up the theme: at first mildly whispered and lightly amusing, the rumor passes from person to person, "Dare I tell you? Don't repeat it!" No one knows its source or whether it is fact or fiction, and no one really cares. Like a growing tempest, the rumor becomes the talk of the town. The storm finally bursts in thunder and lightning; the poor victim is undone and can only surrender.

Tito Gobbi, one of the great Figaros, said of *The Barber of Seville*: "The music gushes forth like a tidal wave, submerging everything. Then as the wave retreats it leaves in its wake a cascade of notes glittering in the sunshine. Rossini gave the opera elegance and humor with the divine, inexhaustible grace of his music."

The first night audience in 1816 did not agree. The choice of Beaumarchais's play proved problematical. The highly respected Giovanni Paisiello (1740–1816), who himself had composed an opera based on the play some years earlier, was still alive. While it was common for different composers to write operas based on the same source, Paisiello's supporters were offended by the young Rossini's temerity in challenging the old master and did all they could to disrupt the first night. There were jeers and catcalls even before the opera began, and a series of stage mishaps didn't help matters. When Count Almaviva, sung by celebrated Spanish tenor Manuel Garcia, sang a Spanish melody under Rosina's balcony, accompanying himself on guitar, the crowd did not approve of the song, and jeered when he broke a string. (In the second performance, Almaviva's lovely aria "Ecco ridente" replaced the Spanish melody.) When Don Basilio tripped over an open trap door, fell, hit his nose, then had to sing "La Calunnia" with a handkerchief held to his face to staunch the bleeding, the audience hissed. Then, during the Act I finale, a cat walked on stage and everyone chased it until it dived under Rosina's skirts. The audience roared. The lively, independent Rosina was not the shrinking violet the audience expected for a girl in her position, and they reacted negatively and noisily to her part in the opera. At the end of the act, as pandemonium broke out in the theatre, only Rossini applauded the singers. When it looked as if Act II would fare no better, he left the chaos and returned home.

The second night, pleading sickness but actually unable to face another hostile audience, Rossini waited in his rooms until he heard Garcia at the head of a crowd outside his window, chanting, "Bravo, bravissimo Figaro!" Without Paisiello's claque, *Il Barbiere de Siviglia*, as the opera came to be called, was a resounding success.

Figaro's creator, Beaumarchais lived a remarkable life. He claimed he wrote plays only for amusement, but through all the trials and tribulations of his life, writing for the theatre remained an essential component of his personality. Like Figaro, Beaumarchais was a "fixer," and held many jobs – from musician to ship owner, from secret agent and gun runner to courtier and man of letters. He was alternately rich and poor, accepted at court and exiled, even imprisoned. He had wanted to write an opera about Figaro, his lively alter ego, but the Opéra Comique turned him down, so Figaro became the key figure of a trilogy of plays: first *Le barbier de Séville*; then *Le mariage de Figaro*, first performed in 1784, and which Mozart transformed into his famous opera only two years later. It was in 1816 that Rossini described Figaro's escapades in his version of *The Barber of Seville*. The third play, *La mère coupable* (The Guilty Mother), became an opera by Darius Milhaud in 1966.

The French king, Louis XVI declared Beaumarchais' second play, *Le mariage de Figaro*, impertinent for its criticism of the aristocracy, and banned its performance.

Figaro, like Beaumarchais, was an impudent adventurer who thumbed his nose at authority and flaunted his opinions; the king was not amused. Only after numerous revisions to satisfy the censor did the play appear, in 1784, when it ran for 68 performances and was a major success; Beaumarchais gave his earnings to charity. Those first, pre-Revolution audiences applauded Beaumarchais as a "courageous man who dared to comment on and ridicule the freedom of the nobility, the ignorance of the magistrates, and the false pleadings of lawyers," reported Gudin, one of Beaumarchais's biographers. Napoleon called the play "revolution in action." Mozart's *Le Nozze di Figaro* appeared in Vienna two years later, again after struggles with the censor – for the Austrian emperor had also banned Beaumarchais's outrageous play about upstart servants outwitting their masters. After a roller coaster career, Beaumarchais died in 1799 in his beloved Paris at the age of 67, when Rossini was seven years old.

Gioacchino Rossini led an equally colorful life – without involvement in state politics but with plenty of operatic intrigues. He was born in Pesaro in 1792 to Giuseppe Rossini, an itinerant trumpeter and horn player, and Anna Guidarini, a soprano with little formal training but a lovely voice and stage personality. Giuseppe, a likable, lively man, was outspoken on behalf of Italy's Republican movement, which led to frequent run-ins with the authorities; he ended up in jail more than once. His life could well have been the subject of one of his son's comic operas. Gioacchino often traveled with his parents during his early years. Music came naturally to him, and he soon found that opera was the form that most appealed to him. The young Rossini had an intuitive feel for humor and a natural facility for composition, and success came early to him. He quickly came to be loved by Italian audiences for both his serious and his comic works, and was much sought after by audiences and managements alike ("Everyone sends for me, everyone calls me," Figaro sings in "Largo al factotum.") Beethoven admired his work, and advised him to "Make more *Barbers*."

In the early 19th century, Italian opera composers wrote two to three operas a year for an opera season that ran from late December through Carnival, a time of revelry, parties and theatre-going and ended with Lent, a time of austerity in the early spring – not a long season, but one that subjected composers, artists, and theatres to extraordinary demands and very short deadlines. After many early successes, *L'Italiana in Algeri,* was the opera which launched Rossini on the road to lasting fame in May 1813. *The Barber of Seville*, Rossini's 17th opera, was composed just before his 24th birthday.

In the winter of 1815, Rossini first presented *Torvaldo e Dorliska* at the Teatro Valle in Rome on 26 December, then turned to composing *The Barber of Seville.* The contract stated that he would write the opera to a libretto provided by the impresario, agree to make any changes requested by the singers, be on hand for rehearsals, and would conduct, from the keyboard, the first three performances. The opera had to be ready and orchestrated by early February to enable the singers to learn their parts, make changes, etc. – an incredibly short deadline, but not unusually so for the time. As soon as the libretto was in his hands – in the last week of January – Rossini got to work and *The Barber* opened at Rome's Teatro Argentina on February 20th. Rossini had composed approximately 600 pages of music in full score in about 15 days!

Beaumarchais's play must have appealed at once to Rossini. Since Beaumarchais had originally planned *Barber* as an opera, the character of Figaro in the play was already a figure of motion, energy, with dialogue that read like music. The librettist, Cesare Sterbini, who had worked with Rossini on *Torvaldo e Dorliska*, stayed close to the Beaumarchais play in writing the libretto for *Almaviva, ossia l'inutile precauzione* (Almaviva, or The Useless Precaution), as the opera was originally titled.

Rossini's *bel canto* style merged well with Beaumarchais's play. In moving away from the strict classicism of the more structured *opera seria* to develop what came to be known as *bel canto* (beautiful singing), Rossini changed the course of 19th-century opera. He said *bel canto* required three elements: a naturally beautiful voice, elaborate technical skills, and the ability to deliver the style with both taste and feeling. The complex structure of Rossini's *buffo* operas allows for all kinds of comedy, from broad slapstick and farce among the characters to a mocking of the operatic form itself, all while maintaining the *bel canto* style.

While *The Barber of Seville* is fun to watch and hear, it is deceptively simple. It demands much of the singers, who, in addition to having to easily and gracefully navigate both the score's turbulent seas and its more lyrical *bel canto* sections, must also be excellent comedic actors. Rossini's extraordinary gift for a bright, brilliant edge in both vocal and instrumental writing, his tight control of musical form, and his fast, quick-witted dialogue or patter, consolidated his genius and ensured his lasting success.

♪

Characters

Figaro, the Barber of Seville	baritone
Count Almaviva	tenor
Rosina, ward of Dr. Bartolo	mezzo-soprano
Dr. Bartolo, Rosina's guardian	bass
Don Basilio, priest and music teacher	bass
Berta, Dr. Bartolo's housekeeper	soprano

Bibliography

Beaumarchais, Pierre-Augustin, *The Barber of Seville* and
The Marriage of Figaro. New York: Penguin Books, 1978.

Gobbi, Tito. *Tito Gobbi on His World of Italian Opera*.
New York: Franklin Watts, 1984.

John, Nicholas, ed. *The Barber of Seville/Moses*, English
National Opera Guide 36. New York: Riverrun Press, 1985.

Osborne, Richard. *Rossini*, Master Musicians series.
Oxford University Press, 2001.

Ainadamar

Osvaldo Golijov

Throughout his life, Federico García Lorca was intrigued with Gypsies, flamenco, and *duende*. The colors and rhythms of the music and songs of Spain permeate his work, and are forcefully expressed again in the score of Osvaldo Golijov's *Ainadamar*. In Lorca's famous lecture "Play and Theory of the Duende," given in Havana in 1934, he said, "These dark sounds are the mystery, the roots thrusting into the fertile earth known to all of us, ignored by all of us, but from which we get the very substance of art." *Duende* can be found "in everything that springs out of the energetic spirit." Goethe, describing *duende* in relation to the music of Paganini, called it a "mysterious power which everyone senses and no philosopher explains." A master guitarist once said, "*Duende* is not in the throat; the *duende* climbs up inside you, from the very soles of the feet," coming to life in the nethermost recesses of the blood, from ancient cultures and creative action.

Lorca spoke of the flamenco singer Pastora Pavon, who, when challenged, "Got up like a woman possessed, her face blasted like a medieval mourner, tossed off a great glass of liquor at a single draught, and began to sing with a scorched throat without voice, without breath, without nuance, but with *duende*! She had contrived to annihilate all that was nonessential in song and make way for an angry and incandescent *duende*, friend of sand-laden winds. How she sang! Her voice jetted up like blood, ennobled by sorrow and sincerity; it opened up like a ten-fingered hand around the nailed feet of a Christ by Juan de Juni."

"All the arts are capable of *duende*," Lorca said. "But where it finds its greatest range, naturally, is in music, dance, and spoken poetry, for these arts require a living body to interpret them, being forms that are born, die, and open their contours in an exact present."

Lorca always used or invoked music in his plays. In the openings of both *Maria Pineda* and *Ainadamar*, a chorus of young girls sings:

> How sad it was in Granada!
> *The stones began to cry;*
> *They could not make Mariana speak,*
> *And so she had to die.*

By the time of his death in 1936, at the age of 38, Lorca was a highly acclaimed playwright and poet in Spain and South America who, in the course of his brief career, had visited New York, Cuba, and Argentina. In the early months of that final year he had declined an invitation from the actress and director Margarita Xirgu, his close friend and collaborator, to go to Mexico to direct his plays. Instead, in mid-July, he left Madrid for his beloved Granada, aware that the political situation was growing increasingly dangerous for him. Since the coming to power of the Second Spanish Republic in 1931, Spain had sunk into political crisis until, in July, the rebel Falangist forces, under the command of Francisco Franco, rose up and attacked. Granada fell on July 18, 1936.

When the fascists came to power, their first actions were to "clean up" cities such as Granada. They came many times to Lorca's parents' house, where he was staying. At last, convinced of the danger, he took refuge in the home of a young poet, Luis Rosales. But Franco's Falangists discovered his hiding place; on August 16, a large-scale operation under the direction of Ramon Ruiz Alonso was mounted to arrest the poet. Alonso, a worker promoted to member of parliament in fascist times, hated Lorca, whom he referred to as "the poet with the big head." When Alonso arrived at her home, Señora Rosales refused him entrance, and asked why he wanted to question Lorca. But Alonso prevailed; Lorca was taken away to government headquarters and imprisoned there. He was accused of having leftist views and for being a subversive writer, a homosexual, and (unjustifiably) a communist. He had once said, "I will always be on the side of those who have nothing and who are not even allowed to enjoy the nothing they have in peace."

In the early hours of August 18, Lorca was taken from the government building, handcuffed to a Republican schoolteacher, and driven to the village of Viznar, northeast of Granada. The following morning, before dawn, Lorca, the teacher, and two bullfighters were taken to the olive groves at Fuente Grande (Big Fountain), a place that the Arabs had named Ainadamar (Fountain of Tears) centuries before. All four were shot, their bodies left by the wayside. Lorca's death uncannily echoed the lines of his own play, *Mariana Pineda*, written many years before:

> *By the edge of the fountain,*
> *When no one was watching,*
> *My hope came to nothing.*

Thereafter, the actual life of Federico García Lorca was quickly transformed into legend and myth. The martyrdom of the young poet and playwright came to symbolize a cruel dictatorship's oppression of the peoples of Spain.

How to present the many aspects of this unique man, and how to unravel fact from fiction and life from legend, presented challenges to composer Osvaldo Golijov and librettist David Henry Hwang when they chose Lorca as the subject of an opera. Golijov believes that Lorca was made a myth by fate; it was this transformation from life to myth that attracted him as a composer.

To describe this transformation, Golijov and Hwang merged three stories: those of Mariana Pineda, a 19th-century liberal heroine of Granada, Spain; of Lorca's own history; and of Margarita Xirgu, the actress and close friend of Lorca's, for whom he wrote many leading roles.

In the 1820s, Mariana Pineda, a young widow in Granada and the mother of two children, was drawn into the world of political opposition through her friends and a cousin, Pedro de Sotomayor, whom she loved; together, they opposed Spain's tyrannical king, Ferdinand VII. When de Sotomayor was imprisoned for acts of treason, Pineda helped him escape. Liberal meetings were held in her house, and she aided other fugitives, protecting them from Ferdinand's police. In March 1831, after the Royalists discovered a liberal flag she had embroidered, Pineda was placed under arrest. Imprisoned in a convent that also held Granada's prostitutes, she stood firm in her refusal to name her fellow conspirators. That May, she was led through the streets and garrotted at the Campo de Triunfo. Her body was buried in a common grave until 1856, when she was reburied in Granada's cathedral, and a statue of her was placed in a square in Granada that was renamed Plaza de Mariana Pineda. Over the years, Pineda's memory was celebrated in ballads that the young Lorca grew up singing. Later, in bringing her back to life in his play *Mariana Pineda*, Lorca, uncannily, predicted his own execution.

When Lorca moved with his family to Granada in 1909 at the age of 11, he lived near the square that contained Mariana's statue and became fascinated by the young woman's story, her courage and sacrifice. She symbolized for him Granada itself, which he loved passionately. He loved her dark sadness, the *duende* of her legend, so imbued with the soul and spirit of Andalusia. The ballads had taught him to believe that Pineda had embroidered the liberal flag as much for love of her cousin as for democracy. "She became a martyr for Liberty being, in reality, a victim of her own enamored and crazed heart," Lorca wrote. In *Mariana Pineda*, Lorca focuses on Mariana's love for Pedro de Sotomayor; for him, she neglects her children and risks her life. But de Sotomayor fails her; when she is arrested, he and his comrades make no attempt to save her. She accepts her fate, faces her final hours with dignity, and dies alone.

Mariana Pineda resonated with Lorca on many levels. Her need for love and her longing for liberty and freedom paralleled his own youthful desires. Lorca could never find true freedom in love because of his homosexuality, which his culture and time demanded be kept hidden; in his plays, heroines suffer unrequited love and male characters fail as lovers. Pineda waits and longs for deliverance that does not come. In Lorca's play *Yerma*, the title character longs for a child but cannot become pregnant; the daughters in his *The House of Bernarda Alba* are driven mad by the strict confinement of their lives; in *Blood Wedding* (Bodas de Sangre), an illicit love affair leads to tragedy. Again and again in Lorca's poems and plays, the dream of love is destroyed and death soon follows. "In every country," Lorca wrote in his lecture on *duende*, "Death comes as a finality. Death comes and they draw the curtains. But not in Spain! In Spain they open them! Many people live out their lives between walls until the day they die and are brought out into the sunlight. In Spain the dead are more alive than the dead of any other country."

Although Lorca was plagued by deep inner sadness and was often chronically depressed, according to people who knew him, he was also a joyous presence, charismatic, with a resonant laugh and gleaming eyes. Still, he was drawn to and repelled by the idea of death. His close friend Salvador Dalí reported that as a student, Lorca would act out his own death, lie his body in a makeshift coffin and describe the process of decomposition.

In writing *Mariana Pineda*, Lorca voiced the fatalism of

the Spanish psyche when he described Pineda's emotional and physical deaths as synonymous. In true Romantic – one could say operatic – fashion, *Mariana Pineda* tells of doomed love, the threatening presence of the villainous police chief (so like Scarpia, the ruthless police chief in Puccini's *Tosca*), the secret meetings, the convent setting, and Pineda's love, longing, abandonment, and execution. Lorca writes mood into these scenes with telling accuracy: the flickering candles in scene i mirror Pineda's fluttering heart, her alternating hopes and fears; in scene ii, the unnerving sound of wind and rain engulf her and her friends and project a sense of imminent danger; finally, the glow that fills the stage at the end gives us a sense of her peace of mind as she faces death. Lorca instructed that this final scene be set "in the extraordinary light of sunset in Granada, a glow of rose and green flowing through the archways. From above comes a soft orange light that grows in intensity to the end of the play." Musically, Golijov connects with Lorca's stage directions and explains, "I wrote an interlude for the guitars and orchestra to symbolize Lorca's wish for a transformation to deep orange in the stage lights."

From the day of Lorca's execution, similar in so many ways to the execution of Mariana Pineda, one person worked ceaselessly for 30 years to keep his memory alive: Margarita Xirgu. Known in the early 20th century as the leading Catalán actress of the Spanish stage, Xirgu developed a political consciousness at an early age. In the choice of plays presented by her company, she exposed corrupt political actions, social discontent, and government injustice. From 1915 to 1936 she based her repertory theatre in Madrid, where she promoted many writers, foremost among them Lorca. They had first met in 1926, when he read *Mariana Pineda* to her company; the following year, she starred in and premiered the play in Barcelona. This first collaboration with Xirgu was to be the beginning of an intense relationship between poet and actress. Xirgu was Lorca's first and favorite Mariana, a role she played countless times, before and after Lorca's death. But while Xirgu loved and promoted Lorca, and was his muse and inspiration, she was never his lover. He said of her, "Margarita Xirgu has the restlessness of the theatre, the fever of multiple temperaments. I always see her at a crossroads, at the crossroad of all heroines, an objective swept by a dark wind where the aorta sings as if it were a nightingale."

In producing *Mariana Pineda*, Xirgu took a risk – the play discussed political beliefs, opinions, and actions, all subjects that were heavily censored by the régime of the time – but the gamble paid off. The play was a great success, and Xirgu, in her portrayal of Pineda, came to be regarded as a social icon who voiced the concerns of the people. As has happened many times throughout history, theatre became one of the few places where ideas and emotions could be at least obliquely expressed, censors notwithstanding.

On tour in South America at the outbreak of the Spanish Civil War, Xirgu decided to remain abroad; until her death in 1969 at the age of 81, she devoted the rest of her life to the theatre of Uruguay, Chile, and Argentina. With the production of Lorca's plays banned in Spain in the years following his death, it was Xirgu who kept his work alive and sowed the seeds of the cult of Lorca that has grown ever since.

Osvaldo Golijov, the composer of *Ainadamar*, was born in La Plata, Argentina; his Jewish grandparents came from Russia and Romania. While Golijov is fully trained in the classical styles of western Europe, his music communicates Klezmer and Gypsy sounds, the tangos and rumbas of South America, along with the mid-European, Moorish, and Spanish influences audible in many of his compositions. Since 1990 he has been closely allied with the Tanglewood Music Center, the summer home of the Boston Symphony, and has written many works for the Kronos Quartet. In 1994 he composed *The Dreams and Prayers of Isaac the*

Blind, which describes a great Kabbalist rabbi of 800 years ago. His *Last Round* (1996) is a tribute to Astor Piazzolla, he has set texts by Pablo Neruda, and in 2000, in a complete departure from earlier works, he composed *The St. Mark Passion*, a retelling of the story of the Crucifixion in music ranging from Latin plainsong to Latin-American and Afro-Caribbean dances.

Golijov composed *Ayre*, a series of 11 songs in Ladino, the language of 15th-century Spanish Jews, for soprano Dawn Upshaw. First performed at Carnegie Hall in March 2004 with the Boston Symphony Chamber Players, the *Ayre* songs are Golijov's new-old arrangements of Arab, Jewish, and Christian folk songs from medieval Spain. Golijov had already created the role of Margarita Xirgu in *Ainadamar* for Upshaw, who sang the first performance at Tanglewood in summer 2003, again at Los Angeles's Walt Disney Concert Hall in 2004, and now in a fully staged version at The Santa Fe Opera, directed by Peter Sellars. (Sellars and Upshaw previously collaborated on the premiere of Kaija Saariaho's *L'Amour de loin* in Santa Fe in 2002.)

In an interview in January 2005, Golijov discussed *Ainadamar* with the author:

Desirée Mays: *What attracted you to Lorca as a subject?*

Osvaldo Golijov: I've loved Lorca since childhood, loved his sensuality, his rhythm, his immensity as an artist.

DM: *What are the challenges of composing an opera and working with a director?*

OG: *Ainadamar* was conceived as a one-act opera, a chamber opera for young voices [at Tanglewood]. The challenge of working with Peter Sellars is great. I love learning from him and arguing with him. He is the kind of artist I need to collaborate with: someone uncompromising. The balance with Peter Sellars will be of creative tension, hopefully yielding blazing beauty.

DM: *How did you collaborate with the librettist, David Henry Hwang? [Hwang is the author of* M. Butterfly *and other plays.]*

OG: Mostly scene by scene. I translated the libretto into Spanish [the language in which the opera is performed]. I molded Hwang's virtuoso English into a Spanish that suits the opera's musical needs. There is a constant interchange between us. I am in awe of David's imagination, his power to synthesize, his "musical" mind – he thinks his developments in counterpoint. The trajectories of all his characters are always kept in motion and converge beautifully at the climactic points, as Bach's lines do.

DM: *The essence of who Lorca was/is seems key to any approach to him. Your thoughts on this?*

OG: Lorca died so young! He was much more than I was able to capture. There were so many sides to him: an avant-garde side, his "Impossible theatre," his incredible ability to assimilate and make his own all modern theatrical and poetic developments and not lose his almost animal connection to the Spanish earth; his ability to cut through styles ranging from his *Cante Jondo* (Deep Song) to his *Poet in New York*. *Ainadamar* presents only one Lorca: the lyrical, the pure child, joyous but with sudden premonitions of untimely death, a gift to humankind.

DM: *There is multi-ethnicity in your score. What do you see as the opera's main dramatic and musical thrust?*

OG: I always envisioned the opera as a floating pomegranate, bleeding melodies [that are] Arab, Christian, and Jewish, the three civilizations that once coexisted in Spain. Lorca said that the greatest error in Spanish history was the expulsion of the Jews and Muslims – [that] from that moment on, Spain became a provincial and chauvinistic society in the centuries that followed. For saying that, he paid with his life. As to the drama, the opera is an attempt on my part to distill a dark lyricism. All folk art forces us to eliminate props and needless pedantry, to reduce ourselves to essentials: pure line and rhythm. Lorca learned that from the Gypsies of Granada, and I learned it from him.

In the first performance of *Ainadamar*, with Dawn Upshaw as Margarita Xirgu, the other roles were sung by young singers from the Tanglewood Vocal Fellows program. In a tradition going back to opera's earliest days, and which continues in some of the operas of Richard Strauss, the male role of Lorca was cast as a mezzo-soprano. Kelley O'Connor, a graduate student at UCLA who bears an uncanny physical resemblance to Lorca, was applauded for her singing of this demanding role, which was described by critics as "strikingly charismatic." O'Connor will again sing Lorca at The Santa Fe Opera.

Ainadamar was still being revised when *Opera Unveiled 2005* went to press; as presented in Los Angles in 2004, the opera was in three sections or movements – *Mariana, Federico*, and *Margarita* – each of which opens with a ballad. The opera is a "memory" piece told in hindsight through the eyes of the aging Margarita Xirgu, who waits in the wings of a theatre to play the role of Mariana Pineda for the last time. As she begins to remember the past, we see her as a young woman with Lorca when they first meet. Lorca tells her that he wrote *Mariana Pineda* not about politics, but because he had fallen in love with Pineda when he was a child. The young Xirgu promises to devote her life to Lorca, and asks him to read *Mariana Pineda* for her company.

In *Federico*, the older Margarita recalls haunting memories of Lorca's execution and death, and blames herself for not being there to help him at the end. She has had to live on, to become his voice in her presentations of his plays. Gunshots are heard and become, in an ingenious and powerful musical transition, the staccato heel beats of flamenco dancers.

In *Margarita*, the ballad becomes a dirge as Margarita's memories converge on one another. She is gently reminded that it is time for her entrance. Time kaleidoscopes as the young and aging Margaritas come together on stage to sing with Lorca. In her last moments, Margarita comes to realize, in the words of Dawn Upshaw, that "She is finally at peace. She understands the reason for living past Lorca for so many years, [understands] what she had to offer." In finding this peace, Margarita comes to meets death with the dignity and calm of Mariana Pineda, the woman whose life she portrayed so vividly throughout most of her acting life.

Time is suspended in *Ainadamar*'s interweaving of the lives and deaths of these three historical figures. Golijov says, "Sometimes the memories that you have of the dead are more alive than those of living people around you, especially when one gets older and the world as you knew it is dead. That world still lives in you. When it's too hard to reinvent that world every day, I think that's when old people let go and die, to join their world once more. That fate eluded Mariana and Lorca, but Margarita lived to an old age to tell their tale."

In the end, *Ainadamar* unravels the legend of Federico García Lorca to reveal him as an individual, a man who loved, suffered, and died, a human being who, in time, became a legend.

Golijov's music for the opera is exciting, filled with the pulsating rhythms of Spain and ranging from the staccato sounds of gunshots that become flamenco beats to the sad lament that Xirgu sings – a quiet rumba accompanied by percussion, woodwinds, and brass. Elements of jazz embedded in the orchestration bring a contemporary touch to Golijov's weaving-together of the three stories, while the many other musical influences express an undertow of deep sadness. Lorca sings an aria that is tonal and plaintive, the vicious Alonso sounds like a flamenco singer out of control,

Moorish themes give way to guitars, and the whole has a flow that mesmerizes. Lorca's own definition of *Cante Jondo* (Deep Song) describes *Ainadamar* as well: "The melody begins, an undulant, endless melody. It loses itself horizontally, escapes from our hands as we see it withdraw from us toward a point of common longing and perfect passion."

Afterword

The Spanish Civil War lasted from 1936 to 1939. Estimates of the number of lives lost in the war run to half a million, 100,000 of whom were executed; many "disappeared" without a trace. The works of Federico García Lorca, an early victim of the war, were banned in Spain until 1954. The site of his burial was identified only in 1971, when Irish writer Ian Gibson went to Granada to investigate the mystery of his death. Plans to exhume the body believed to be Lorca's are underway, though his family would prefer his remains be left in peace. The controversy over Lorca's exhumation was still unresolved as of January 2005.

Characters

Margarita Xirgu	soprano
The young Margarita	soprano
Federico García Lorca	mezzo-soprano
Ramon Ruiz Alonso	tenor-cantaor
José Tripaldi	baritone

Bibliography

Bach, Caleb. "Composer of Spiritual Communions." *Américas Magazine*, April 2003.

Braun, William. "Act Two: Dawn Upshaw." *Opera News*, June 2004.

Delgado, Maria M. "The Author of Authors: Margarita Xirgu." *"Other" Spanish Theatres*. Manchester University Press, 2003.

Edwards, Gwynne, trans., intro. *Lorca: Plays Three*. Essex, UK: Methuen Publishing Ltd., 2003.

Gibson, Ian. *Federico García Lorca: A Life*. New York: Pantheon Books, 1989.

Kolbert, Elizabeth. "Looking for Lorca." *The New Yorker*, December 22 & 29, 2003.

Maurer, Christopher, ed. *In Search of Duende*. London: New Directions Publishing Corp., 1998. Includes "Play and Theory of Duende," a lecture given by F. G. Lorca in Buenos Aires in 1933.

Ross, Alex. "Deep Song." *The New Yorker*, September 1, 2003.

Lucio Silla

Wolfgang Amadeus Mozart

The end of the 18th century – the years of Mozart – was a time of profound societal transition. The absolute rule of monarchy and church began to give way to the Age of Enlightenment or Reason, a time in which Nature, the individual, and feeling came into their own. The marital fidelity of women became a major topic of interest as the role of women began to change – from the status of mere chattel and bargaining chip in the combining of states and estates, to being the embodiment and keeper of the new moral standards by which society found itself functioning. In these years of revolution in Europe and America, women took on the role of constancy and steadfastness at home, providing anchors and firm bases from which men could roam freely, conducting business and politics as they chose. Still, the dream of the right of liberty and justice for all, with the pursuit of happiness within the theoretical reach of even the most humble, had a long way to go before becoming reality.

The very meaning of the word *constancy* was undergoing change. The Enlightenment redefined and relocated morality to the domestic sphere; women became guardians of society's virtues, specifically those virtues relating to sexual continence. The French philosopher Jean-Jacques Rousseau stated that chastity was the greatest virtue to which a woman could aspire, but this statement contained a hidden agenda: As long as women remained chaste and faithful to their husbands, the sticky question of property inheritance could be safeguarded. Dr. Johnson was more direct: "Consider of what importance to society the chastity of women is. Upon that all the property of the world depends." Eighteenth-century moralists – all men, of course – argued that while sexual promiscuity or infidelity in a man could be viewed as a misdemeanor, in a woman the same behavior was a crime and a sin. Thus the notorious double standard of the time. "The woman who allowed her virtue to slip fatally undermined the stability of society," comments Nicholas Till in his book *Mozart and the Enlightenment*.

Mozart's operas reflect this dilemma. In *The Magic Flute*, the patriarch Sarastro tells the frightened Pamina, "By man your course must be decided, for by herself a woman steps beyond her sphere and is misguided." Yet the "enlightened" emphasis on female constancy required that this fidelity be subjected to the occasional test. It is the faithful and sorely tested Pamina whom Mozart raises – for her constancy and love – to equal status with Tamino. *La Finta Giardiniera* (1775), which follows *Lucio Silla* (1772) in Mozart's oeuvre, focuses on Sandrina, a noblewoman disguised as a gardener whose virtue is tested throughout the opera. When threatened by the Mayor, who sees her as fair game because she is a servant, she repulses him, reminding him that she has a heart, a mind, and feelings. Later abducted and terrorized, Sandrina passes these trials with her virtue intact, insisting that the dignity of her feelings be respected. Mozart himself, who at the time was wincing under the tyrannical rule of the Archbishop of Salzburg, insisted, "I have but to consult my own feelings and judgment [on matters of moral conscience]. It is the heart that ennobles a man, and though I am no count, yet I probably have in me more honor than in many a count." Years later, another servant girl – and this time not a noblewoman in disguise – fights to maintain her virtue: Susanna, in *The Marriage of Figaro*.

Mozart knew what it was to be a servant; he was treated as one of the lowliest in the Archbishop's court. This must have rankled a young man who had grown used to receiving the respect of the crowned heads of Europe, and whose father, Leopold, had taught him that a man's dignity was paramount. Among the many servants in Mozart's operas one finds the flamboyant and wily Figaro, and Leporello, the voice of conscience for his philandering master, Don Giovanni. In *Così fan tutte*, the servant Despina acts as advisor to her vulnerable mistresses, Fiordiligi and Dorabella, when their constancy is tested – tests those sisters fail miserably. The ultimate test comes in *The Magic Flute*, when Pamina must pass a series of terrifying physical trials. She triumphs – not by following Tamino through the trials, but by taking him by the hand and leading him through them.

In Mozart's *Zaide*, the constant woman appears in another guise: that of muse. This opera, which had many autobiographical connections to Mozart's own situation at the time, tells of a slave, Gomatz who, it has been suggested, is Mozart himself. (Mozart, a lover of word games and cryptic puzzles, connected the name *Gomatz* with his own: change one letter and *Gomatz* becomes *Romatz*, an anagram for *Mozart*.) When Gomatz falls into an exhausted sleep, Zaide, the Sultan's favorite, appears before him to offer hope and consolation. The slave master, Allazim, turns out to be Gomatz's father, and both are slaves of the Sultan. The father accepts his servitude, as did Leopold Mozart, (in his position as kapellmeister to the Archbishop of Salzburg) and the son ever resists it, as did Wolfgang.

Mozart never finished *Zaide*, but reworked it into *Die Entführung aus dem Serail*, in which the heroine, Constanze, sings heroically of her preference of death over infamy. Eighteenth-century female characters such as Constanze, venerated as paragons of virtue, were perceived to have the power to redeem not only themselves and their beloveds but, on occasion, entire societies. By the 19th century this shift from women as upholders of moral values in the domestic sphere to those with the power to redeem on a larger scale was a crucial elenent in what became the full-blown Romantic movements in art, music, and poetry, culminating in the great love-torn operas of Wagner and his heroines Senta, Elisabeth, and Brünnhilde.

Mozart composed a number of operas that bridged the Classical and Romantic eras most of which, in one way or another, addressed the issue of woman's constancy. In *Mitridate, re di Ponto* (1770), Aspasia and Ismene, both daughters of kings, hold out amid the political maneuverings of the men surrounding them; in *Idomeneo* (1781), Ilia, a captive princess, offers herself as sacrifice to the gods in place of the man she loves. Ilia is *Idomeneo's* only "enlightened" character – only she sees beyond the old ways of man's relationship to the gods. Her sacrifice is validated when Neptune himself steps in to prevent her death and applaud her thesis of "Love triumphs."

The popularity of the opera seria style was beginning to wane during Mozart's lifetime. *La Clemenza di Tito* (1791), composed for the coronation in Prague of Leopold II, is the last great example. The heroic style had served well the needs of the aristocracy at a time when absolute monarchy was law. This form of entertainment was one whose elite audience was concerned not with mere men but with heroes; the stories, derived from the Greek and Roman classics, had to present monarchs who, in the end, always tempered justice with mercy. Opera seria was symbolic, artificial and ceremonially stylized – all reasons for its demise and lack of appeal to 19th-century audiences, for whom, following vast social upheavals, the classical plots were no longer relevant or of interest.

Mozart, as a very young composer, had to write in the form of opera seria, a formal, structured style in which stereotypical characters were easily recognized by the audience. Entrances and exits were strictly regulated. The action, or storytelling part of the plot was advanced by recitatives, in which a single instrument would accompany the vocal line. The arias were called "da capo" in which one melody introduced the aria, followed by a middle section, then a return to the beginning (da capo: the head) for repeats with much vocal embellishments and decorations, runs, trills, cadenzas.

An opera seria was expected to conclude – regardless of what had gone before – with a king's magnanimous gesture. Mitridate dies forgiving his sons, whom he had previously condemned to death; Idomeneo abdicates in favor of his son Idamante, whom he was about to sacrifice; in *La Clemenza di Tito*, the king forgives all the conspirators in an extraordinary act of clemency; and in *Lucio Silla*, the Emperor abdicates.

For the young Mozart, composing before the French Revolution, much was changing in his personal life in these years. By 1772, his career as a child prodigy was over without securing an appointment to a major European court – as his father had hoped. Mozart was faced with the unhappy prospect of living his life in the service of the Archbishop of Salzburg, whom he intensely disliked. Mozart viewed Salzburg, the city of his birth, as provincial, a place where there was no possibility of fulfilling his musical destiny. Despite this, he composed prolifically during his years at the Archbishop's beck and call; he loved opera seria above all else, and in a letter to his father wrote, "Don't forget my wish to write operas! But it must be in Italian, not German, and opera seria, not buffa."

In addition to Mozart's poor job prospects, there was mounting tension between father and son. Leopold's expectations of Wolfgang were excessive; he attempted to dictate every aspect of his son's life, from personal behavior and decisions to dress, thoughts, and friends. The two were still musical collaborators in the early 1770s, but by the time of *Die Entführung aus dem Serail* in 1782, Mozart had moved away from parental control and rarely consulted his father for advice of any kind.

During his teenage years Mozart was aware of Enlightenment ideas about nature and the individual, as well as of the changes taking place within himself; the music of *Lucio Silla* expresses his awakening to romantic feeling. He had always been attracted to women – as a child, he was fêted by the ladies of the royal courts of Europe, he adored his mother and sister, and in his adolescent years enjoyed playful relationships with cousins and many young female friends. He respected women, and throughout his musical career explored the issue of constancy. He even married a woman named Constanze, and wrote in a letter to his father of "my dearest Constanze! She is not ugly, but one could not call her a beauty. Her whole beauty consists of two black eyes and a graceful figure. She has no wit, but wholesome common sense enough to fulfill her duties as wife and mother. She has the kindest heart in the world and I love her and she me with all our hearts! Tell me if I could wish myself a better wife?" Constanze's virtue and domesticity provided Mozart with the affection and stability for which he longed.

Mozart and Leopold enjoyed their tours to Italy and even hoped for an appointment at the Court of Archduke Ferdinand, but it was not to be. When Mozart and his father returned to Salzburg after such a tour in 1771, they learned that the Archbishop had died and was to be succeeded by the worldly Archbishop Colloredo who agreed to give Mozart a small annual salary. Mozart and Leopold set out once again in October 1772 to fulfil a contract for a new opera in Milan. Mozart had no say in the choice of subject when he received the commission for this opera; *Lucio Silla* was simply assigned to him, as was the custom of the day. Giovanni de Gamerra, whose libretto for *Lucio Silla* was only his second, followed the tradition of Metastasio, the court poet at Vienna, on whose works the majority of opera seria were set.

Lucio Silla meets all the criteria of opera seria. A classic tale set in Rome in 80 B.C., it is loosely based on the life of the historical Lucius Sulla, a Roman soldier who marched on Rome at a time of civil unrest in 88 B.C. Later, when he went to fight in Asia Minor, Sulla left Cinna in charge of Rome as Consul. On his return, he had to retake Rome by force, and became its Dictator in 82 B.C., killing his opponents and banishing or executing those senators and noblemen who opposed him. The opera presents the classic interweaving of affairs of state – the conspiracy to overthrow Sulla, which was based on fact – with fictional affairs of the heart.

Lucio Silla also follows opera seria's structured musical requirements. It includes 18 arias, one duet, one trio, and three ensembles, castrati singing female roles, and women singing male roles. (In Santa Fe, the cast will include a tenor, Lucio Silla; a mezzo-soprano singing a male role, Cecilio; a male soprano, Cinna; and two sopranos, Giunia and Celia.) The arias are interspersed with recitatives accompanied by both *secco* (dry) – that is, with simple chords and arpeggios from the harpsichord – as well as by solo obbligato recitatives from the horns, oboes, and violins.

The opera has five characters: a pair of lovers, the figure of authority who opposes them, and a secondary pair of lovers. Respectively, these are the banished Roman senator, Cecilio, and his wife, Giunia; Lucio Silla, Dictator of Rome; and Silla's sister, Celia, who is in love with Cinna. The opera opens with a miniature three-movement overture that, as was then the custom, relates in no way to the opera.

Act I opens in Rome, by the Tiber River, a place of trees

and ruins. Cecilio has returned secretly from banishment and here meets his friend, Cinna, who tells him that Silla has told Cecilio's wife, Giunia, that her husband is dead. Cinna goes on to say that the mourning Giunia often goes to a cemetery to pray at the grave of her father, whom Silla also had killed, and suggests that Cecilio go there to meet her. In scene ii, Silla asks his sister, Celia, to intercede for him with Giunia, whom he loves. Celia leaves as Giunia enters to tell Silla, in no uncertain terms, how much she loathes him for killing her father and her husband: "Villain, you alone are the object of my hate." Silla is furious that a mere woman should defy him thus, but still loves her. Scene iii takes us to the graveyard vault, where the waiting Cecilio hides as Giunia enters with her attendants. At her father's urn, they pray to the spirits of the dead to rise up against the tyrant Silla. Cecilio steps forward and Giunia gasps, convinced he is a ghost. When she realizes he is alive, the two sing joyously of their love. This scene is quite beautiful – it moves from the deep pathos of Giunia's mourning for her father in a tomb to the miraculous appearance of her husband, and concludes Act I with an ecstatic duet.

In Act II, Silla is advised to take Giunia as his wife, for both she and her dead father remain popular with the people. Cecilio appears, sword in hand, and attempts to follow Silla but is restrained by Cinna, who convinces him that he will put Giunia at great risk if he attacks Silla. Cecilio concedes the truth of this and leaves. Celia enters and tries to tell Cinna of her love for him, but he, more concerned with destroying Silla, is unresponsive. Cinna later tells Giunia that the Senate is about to approve her marriage to Silla and suggests that she kill the Dictator that night. She refuses. Left alone, Cinna swears that he himself will murder the tyrant. At last, in scene iii, which is set in the Capitol, Silla formally asks the Senate to give him Giunia's hand in marriage. She vehemently rejects his proposal and, when Cecilio rushes in, Silla orders that husband and wife be arrested. Silla vents his fury at both: "Such unshakable constancy, such true love, tear at my heart and set me afire."

Act III's prison setting is reminiscent of Beethoven's *Fidelio*, another opera about woman's constancy. Giunia and Cecilio, sure they are about to die, sing tender farewells to each other. In the final scene, the senate and the people wait for Silla to pronounce the sentence of death. But to their amazement, he decrees that Cecilio and Giunia be set free. Furthermore, he gives his sister, Celia, in marriage to Cinna. Finally, he declares, "I am no longer Dictator. I have seen that innocence and a virtuous heart are more pleasing than false splendor," and the opera ends happily. However unsatisfactory and unconvincing, the plot's unlikely but predictably rosy outcome left the first-night audience happy.

Mozart had been given a leave of absence from the Archbishop of Salzburg to go to Milan at the beginning of November 1772 to produce *Lucio Silla*. The principal singers showed up one by one in the ensuing weeks; Mozart had to await their arrivals before he could write their arias, as all of their music had to be composed specifically for their voices. He had an outstanding Cecilio in the castrato Venanzio Rauzzini and a superb Giunia in soprano Anna de Amicus, a singer of considerable talent and expressiveness. Giunia is without question the most developed character in the opera, in part because Mozart clearly sympathized with the unhappy heroine, and partly because in de Amicus he had a superb soprano who was capable of singing every musical challenge he wrote for her, in arias that ranged from bravura coloratura à la the Queen of the Night when she rages at Silla, to virtuoso moments of great tenderness and sadness, to the sensuousness of her duet with Cecilio. Mozart was delighted by her singing of his arias, which he described as "unusual, absolutely unique and extremely difficult."

Rehearsals began in mid-December. The tenor hired to sing Silla had to be replaced at the last moment by a member of a church choir, a man with little stage experience and a merely adequate voice. Mozart had to compose easier replacement arias for him and cut some entirely; ever since, the downsizing of the title role has been problematical for this opera. (Unfortunately, the original arias have not survived.) Final rehearsals took place December 19–24, 1772, and the premiere was held December 26 in the Teatro Regio Ducal, the forerunner of La Scala in Milan.

Not all went well that first night. The performance began hours late because the guest of honor, Archduke Ferdinand, was late. The substitute tenor overacted and upset the prima donna, who did not sing well for the rest of the evening. She was further incensed when the castrato's (Cecilio's) first entrance was greeted by applause from the court members. (Later, it was revealed that the castrato, Rauzzini, had told the Archduchess beforehand that he needed encouragement if he was to sing well.) Despite these upsets, *Lucio Silla* was a success. The premiere performance lasted six hours, and included three ballets, also composed by Mozart, in the intermissions (the ballets have long since been cut). The opera ran to full houses for 26 performances during Carnival. That it was completed at all in such a short time, a little over a month, was a miracle by any standard.

While remaining true to the opera seria form in *Lucio Silla*, Mozart gave the work an atypically dramatic relevance. He built on and extended the traditional da capo form with a series of variations. In Giunia's final recitative and aria, "Fra i pensier" (Filled with melancholy), he even leaves the da capo form behind. The long recitative, accompanied by the orchestra, leads into an aria of extraordinary beauty and intensity in a minor key, the music expressing an emotional maturity well beyond Mozart's youthful years as it accelerates from a heartfelt *andante* to a quick *allegro*, and ends without the expected repeats and decorated passages.

Lucio Silla was the last work of Mozart's to be commissioned and composed in Italy. Following the opening performances, he returned to Salzburg, where he stayed until finally cutting his ties with his native city in 1781 to go to Vienna, where he lived for the remaining ten years of his life. Today, this work is remembered as an early masterpiece of a young composer on the threshold of manhood, for Mozart was only 16 years of age when he composed *Lucio Silla*.

Characters

Lucio Silla, Dictator of Rome	tenor
Cecilio, exiled Roman senator	soprano
	(mezzo-soprano in Santa Fe)
Giunia, wife of Cecilio	soprano
Cinna, a Roman patrician	soprano
	(male soprano in Santa Fe)
Celia, sister of Silla, in love with Cinna	soprano
Aufidio, tribune and friend of Silla	tenor

Bibliography

Mersmann, Hans, ed. *Letters of Mozart.* New York: Dorset Press, 1986.

Osborne, Charles. *The Complete Operas of Mozart.* New York: Da Capo Press, 1978.

Till, Nicholas. *Mozart and the Enlightenment: Truth, Virtue, and Beauty in Mozart's Operas.* New York: W. W. Norton & Co., 1992.